Stand Tall

Stand Tall

Bill Sanders

Fleming H. Revell
A Division of Baker Book House
Grand Rapids, Michigan 49506

Copyright © 1992 by Bill Sanders
Published by Fleming H. Revell,
a division of Baker Book House
P.O. Box 6287, Grand Rapids, MI 49516-6287
Printed in the United States of America

Library of Congress Cataloging-in-Publication Data

Sanders, Bill.
    Stand tall / Bill Sanders
    p.   cm.
    Summary: Guidance with a Christian emphasis for teens who need help with their self-esteem.
    ISBN 0-8007-5452-2
    1. Teenagers—Religious life. 2. Self-esteem—Religious aspects—Christianity—Juvenile literature. [1. Self-esteem. 2. Christian life.] I. Title.
BV4531.2.S26   1992
248.8'3—dc20   92-13985
                                          CIP
                                          AC

To the special people who have helped me to accept myself as the marvelous miracle whom God made (faults and all), to search for the truth of my past, and to realize that I have worth because God made me that way.

Thanks, Mom, for sharing so openly and honestly with me. It's so nice to call you friend.

Kathryn, your insights and gentle encouragement for me to seek and speak the truth have been lifesaving.

My children, you have had great love and patience waiting for me to show how Jesus would have been a dad.

Jimbo, you are always there to listen, encourage, and grow with me.

Kevin, thanks for teaching me that it's okay to need to be needed.

Holly, as always, you are my greatest supporter and friend.

Mary and Jean, you both have lovingly encouraged me to honestly look at myself and life. Thank you!

And to my longtime colleague and friend Gary Thompson. You have spent months helping me put this book together. Without your love, friendship, wisdom, and knowledge, it would never have been completed.

Contents

Preface
A Winning Combination

Did you ever . . . wish you could feel better about yourself? . . . Feel your world is falling apart? . . . Think your self-image has gotten so muddy that you don't even know what you look like?

If so, this book is for you.

I've written *Stand Tall* to help you look at yourself, your world, and your emotions. What makes you feel the way you do about yourself? How can you change the things you don't like? How do you make the most of your strong points? Can you even hope when everything looks rotten?

Hundreds of days each year I speak to teens, parents, and teachers in schools across the nation. I tell adults what it's like to be a teen and try to explain adults to teens. Then I show each why the other is important and how they can understand and communicate better.

While I'm in schools, I listen to teens, and after I leave, I often hear from them. Every week young people send me letters like this one:

Dear Bill:
    I hate life. No one cares for me—not even my parents. Mom and I get along some of the time, but my dad has abused me a lot. I wish I had another family.

Neither of my parents likes my new boyfriend—in fact they haven't liked any of my boyfriends.

My dog just died, too.

Why does God hate me? He must hate me to allow this to happen.

I really liked your talk the other day at our school, but now I feel extra bad, because the only time I feel good is when I'm having sex with my boyfriend, and you've told me that is wrong.

Will I ever have bright days? Can I get a better outlook? How can I learn to feel good about myself? I've tried, Bill, by praying and asking God to help, as you suggested, but he doesn't seem to be there for me. No one seems to answer.

Please help me, I'm desperate. You are my last hope. If you don't write back, I'll understand.

Signed,

Hurting

I feel Hurting's pain. After all, I remember when I was a tall, awkward, self-conscious teen who felt he didn't match up to people's standards. I agonize with her and the others who send me such messages; frequently I send them books and tapes that offer practical help and try to provide them with long-term support.

Once in a while I get back letters that report: "I followed the steps you gave me, and it worked. Though I have my tough days, I'm stepping out and doing the things that help me feel good about myself. I really do feel great now. For the first time in my life, I feel whole." Then every ounce of effort I've put into the assemblies, the letters, and each page of every book I've written seems well worth it.

Maybe today you feel as if you could have written a hurting and hopeless letter. If so, I want to help you learn to love life, have hope instead of despair, and look at the bright side, instead of falling into a hole of pain.

As you read, I hope you feel as if I were sitting with you in your home or standing next to you at your locker. Let me share from my heart and my experience—and from the stories of hundreds of young people who have hurt when they've done things that don't work but have found joy in turning life around.

I haven't lectured you on how to feel happy, because I know that won't help much. I have given you ideas I've seen work; then I've tried to show you how to put them in your life by sharing the stories of some teens who have used my tips. Though the names and some of the particulars are changed, to protect their privacy, I haven't altered the main truths. When I tell you one person's story, you can count on the fact that hundreds of other teens out there have shared the same problem. They have felt pain and have found hope. None of them had advantages you don't have.

Slowly read the ideas I'll give you and think about them. Underline the steps that mean the most to you. Share some of what you learn with a friend. Put these tips to work in your life, because they can help.

How can I say that so confidently? Not only have I seen these ideas work for teens, I know they will pass the test of time because they are more than my own inventions. God made us for happiness, not to feel miserable about ourselves. To show us how to live with joy, he gave us the Bible. From that source and the experiences of people who have walked close to him, I have developed these ideas.

God and I care about you. Join forces with us, and we'll form an unbeatable team that can bring you through any trouble.

PART 1

What It Means to Have Self-esteem

1

Who Am I—Really?

Don't you have any self-esteem?" Jack's dad cried at him one day. The teen felt confused. Sure he'd forgotten to take out the garbage, but what did that have to do with the issue?

Sixteen-year-old Todd was accused of a series of burglaries. After meeting with Todd's mother, a social worker commented, "He wouldn't be a bad kid if he had any self-esteem."

Cynthia's best friend overheard a teacher say, "Cynthia really has leadership potential, but I don't think she'll do much until she feels better about herself."

We've all heard about self-esteem, but do we know what it is? What's behind all the blame placing and talk?

Finding Self-esteem

Webster's *New Collegiate Dictionary* calls self-esteem "A confidence and satisfaction in oneself: self-respect." We don't need to kiss ourselves in the mirror every morning and act as if no one could match up to us in order to have self-esteem; that's not self-esteem—it's conceit. We do need to respect ourselves, our abilities, and our own futures.

You may try to hide the truth from yourself about how you feel you rate, but you can't squirrel it away from others. The way you act will show your inner thoughts all the time. Do you put drugs into your body? Then you don't respect yourself. Do you see yourself as a loser? Then you will treat yourself as if everyone should kick you—and some people will.

When I speak at an assembly, I can tell right away which teens think they are of value and which are filled with self-doubt. Those who want to learn and have a positive outlook about themselves sit right down in front. Most of them have had others tell them they are worthwhile achievers and contributors to the school. They don't feel that they have to hide in the back of the gym.

Others dress as if they are not special and look as if they need showers and haircuts. They head for the far corner in the back row. Because they don't expect much from the assembly, they don't get much out of it, and their behavior pictures their opinions of themselves.

Look at Yourself

Another word closely related to *self-esteem* is *self-image*. While self-esteem describes how you think about yourself, self-image is the value you place on what you see. Webster's says it's "one's conception of oneself or one's role."

You might think of it this way: First you see yourself. Are you talented or stupid, confident or doubtful? How you answer that describes your self-image. From that perception, you give yourself a value—you decide if you are good or bad—that's self-image.

Danny misses an answer in a verbal math quiz. *I'm dumb,* he decides, and in Danny's family it's important to be smart. So he decides he's bad because he can't live up to his parents' values. That afternoon he goes home and picks a fight with his brother. When Danny felt bad about his mistake, his self-esteem plummeted. That made him label himself *bad*. Now he had a poor self-image. His actions showed his emotions when he took out his pain on his brother.

Naturally we all have days when we don't see ourselves as being very valuable. When you feel sick, you have an argument with your best friend, or if you realize just as you get to English class that today you have a quiz you didn't study for, you may feel down. Still, you don't need to feel that way every day.

How do you most often feel about yourself? Get some clues from "The Self-esteem Quiz."

The Self-esteem Quiz

I usually:

T F Know that God loves me.

T F Think that my parents wish I'd never been born.

T F Feel I'm pretty special to my family.

T F Wish I had a friend to whom I could talk.

T F Realize that friends love me, even when I don't see them often.

T F Feel as if I'm perfect.

T F Think that no one can do as well as I can in school.

T F Wonder why any of the girls (or guys) in my school would want to go out with me.

T F Wonder why anyone would turn down a date with me.

T F Know that unless I do every assignment perfectly, my teachers will not like me.

T F Will ask questions in class because I want more information. There is no stupid question.
T F Understand that we all make mistakes, but that we can be forgiven.
T F Know that I am made for greatness.
T F Believe I can love others successfully.
T F Let others see my inner beauty.

Do your inner attitudes show that you are hard on yourself? You need to ease up on yourself if you:

- Believe you always need to be perfect
- Doubt God's love for you, even though you have faith that he died for your sins
- Think everyone on earth wishes you'd never been born
- Blame yourself for family problems you can't control

Or maybe you have decided that you are better than others and:

- Think everyone should look up to you
- Treat others as if they owed you service
- Expect everyone to do you favors

If either of these descriptions fits you, you have a problem with self-esteem. People show their poor opinions of themselves in different ways; that doesn't mean one is perfect and the other is flawed. Poor self-esteem comes in lots of different packages. The perfectionist who cannot allow himself to fail has just as big a problem as the conceited beauty queen or the self-effacing student who won't speak up in class.

Problems with self-esteem come in all shapes and sizes—and all personality styles. No one has a perfect opinion of himself or herself, simply because no one is perfect. We tend to hide the hurts and think poorly of ourselves because we can't admit that we have failed. Each of us has a self-esteem problem that needs conquering.

The good news is that we don't have to hide our hurts and take them out on ourselves and others. People are improvable models. By learning from our past mistakes and discovering new ways of attacking our problems, we can have new hope—and new lives.

A New View of Self-esteem

Why do we have problems with self-esteem? Maybe it's because we so often fall for Satan's definition of it. His lie tells us:

Self-esteem = What you do and look like from the outside + How others accept you, praise you, need you, and love you

God has a different equation:

Self-esteem = Your uniqueness + Your relationship with God

While Satan and the world look at the outside stuff, God says, "I love you for who you are, a special person whom I made in a fearful, wonderful way. I died for you and have a plan for your life."

Sure, when you do things well, you feel good—you're wired like that by God, so you will help others instead of staying in your shell. Nonetheless, your value doesn't depend on what you do, how many people like you, or what you wear, as Satan would have you believe. Performance cannot make you acceptable. When others like you, praise you, and notice you, you're no better than before. If they don't notice you, you aren't any worse. That's all outside stuff.

A boy once told me he was ready to commit suicide. Why? Because the college his parents wanted him to go to had just turned him down, and he didn't know how to tell them. Instead of facing them with the truth and finding a school that was better for him, he thought of destroying himself completely. Outside stuff had really gotten to him.

The One and Only You

Don't tie yourself up in looking good or trying to live up to the expectations of others, because it's a dead-end street. Instead, let God's equation for self-esteem free you. Realize that you alone have your thumbprints. Only you have the talents that are part of your makeup—in just the right mix. No one else has your voice. *You* are unique. God made you that way and loves you just as you are—warts and all.

Who are you—really? Just the person God wants to have a relationship with. He wants to be close to you, to have you know him well, and to give you life with him forever. Are you important? You bet! Even on your down days, he's your friend. Turn to him every moment of every day, because you are special.

2

What Influences Self-esteem?

If self-esteem describes how you think about yourself, where did your opinion come from? How did you get where you are today?

Many people's opinions and lots of experiences went into the ideas you have about yourself. Every day the world you live in tells you where you've failed or excelled when it comes to your performance, attitudes, and possessions. People may give you the feeling you are the best person in the world—or the most unimportant.

When you hear messages about yourself, they may come from four sources:

Family attitudes. How your family sees you and the messages it has given you about yourself.

Self-imposed pressures. Ideas of your own that compel you to take certain actions.

Others' expectations. What others think about you or what you think they think about you that causes you to act certain ways.

Hope for the future. Your view of where you're going and how good life will be for you.

How do each of these make you feel bad or good about yourself? Let's see.

What Does My Family Tell Me?

To understand yourself, consider what you have seen day by day at home. The environment you've grown up in strongly influences how you see yourself and others, because from it you learned how to handle—or avoid—problems.

- Does your family say, "I love you," easily, often, and freely? When you say it, do you really mean it?
- Does your family hug one another?
- How does your family show love? Is it hard to do that?
- When you were a child, did your mom and dad hold you in their laps, read to you, sing with you, spend time with you, and tell and show you that you were loved?
- Do you feel comfortable going to your mom and dad and talking about serious problems?
- Are your parents there for you when you share with them, or do you find it easier to hold the pain inside, because you fear their reactions?
- Do your parents seem to like another brother or sister better than you?
- Do your parents constantly compare you to a brother or sister?
- Did you feel wanted or loved during your childhood?
- Have your parents given you the feeling that they did not want you, that you were a mistake?
- Have you been abused—sexually, physically, emotionally, or verbally—by a family member or stranger?
- Does your family seem to need you?
- Do you feel truly important—that without you, your family would be less special?

- Have you helped make some family decisions?
- Would you describe your childhood as happy, sad, or painful?

Once you've answered these questions, you may have an idea that you lived in a really good home—or one that had a lot of troubles. Understand that no matter what you've had, because it's all you know, it will seem "normal."

If you grew up in a home destroyed by alcoholism, that will seem "normal" to you, but it still won't seem right. Embarrassment makes you want to hide the fact that your mom or dad had a drinking problem. You may decide that the way to avoid sorrow is to put on a happy face, so you become everyone's favorite comedian—while you hide your hurt inside.

If you grew up in a family that expressed love easily and went through tough times together, you may not understand what the problem is with other families. You'll expect everyone to have a family as normal as yours, and you may find it hard to understand why other teens seem to think they aren't valuable to their parents, brothers, and sisters.

If you have a good family life, thank God for it. Your parents weren't perfect, but they gave you a warm home. Do all you can to make your family even better. Then reach out and share your love with others.

If you come from a home that lacked love, take heart. Freedom comes when you realize that you cannot control your family situation. You cannot change your parents' mistakes, and you had nothing to do with any pain they inflicted upon you. Refuse to carry the blame and guilt.

Instead, begin to take control of your life, where possible. If you feel depressed all the time, instead of experiencing some "down" times that come with specific problems, seek out a trained counselor who can help you understand your feelings and share with you from God's Word, the Bible.

Sarah told me about her experience with her jealous mother. This teen could hardly go out of the house without hearing her mother's complaints follow her out the door. Sarah never got in trouble when she left home—she simply wanted to spend a little time with friends. Because she had never done anything to cause her mother to be worried, Sarah didn't understand. Was God punishing her for something?

As it turned out, the problem did not lie with Sarah, but with her mother. Mrs. Montrose had married at sixteen, and her marriage had ended in divorce. Now Sarah was sixteen, too, and her mother was reacting in anger. When she looked at the teen, she blamed her daughter for her own missed-out-on childhood, the lost opportunity for a college education, and the other things that an early marriage had denied her. Though she didn't realize it consciously, Mrs. Montrose kept Sarah at home so she would not get pregnant, too.

Sadly, Mrs. Montrose will not accept help for her concealed pain; she resists change. Fortunately, that does not mean Sarah has no hope. Instead of running away from home to get rid of the problems, Sarah has wisely decided to stay for a few more years. Though she cannot change the problems, she has altered the way she thinks about them. Sarah cares for her mother, even when she plays tricks on Sarah, but this teen does not buy into the hurt anymore.

"I understand that you are hurting," she told her mother. "But I am not responsible for what happened before I was born. If you need help, I'll provide any that I can, but I also have my own life." She went on to convince her mom that she would not get pregnant; instead she planned on making the right choices. Realizing the influence her mother's poor self-image had on her view of herself, Sarah began to change her thought patterns and carved out her own successful junior and senior years.

Family has a powerful influence on you, but it does not have the last word. Love them, even when it seems hard, but don't let your parents, brothers, or sisters manipulate you or put you down.

How Do I Pressure Myself?

Though we often don't have much control over our family situations, we do have some say in the pressures we put on ourselves. It's up to us if we'll become reactors, who only go with the flow, or initiators, who make things happen. Do you value what's good and right for you, or do you make yourself do what you think others want?

Susie's father was very unhappy with his marriage, so he avoided arguments by never spending time at home. To build up his hurting self-esteem, he did more than the next guy at work. That meant he spent many hours in the office—and few with Susie. He built his life on the good opinion of his boss and avoided getting close to his family.

When Susie started dating, at thirteen, she did not have a good model to build on, so she did what "everyone" did. By sixteen she had already had four boyfriends—each only after sex.

Deep down, Susie knew her boyfriends did not love her.

"Why do you do it, then?" I asked.

"It may not be right for me to have sex with them, and I know it won't last forever, but night after night, year after year, I've wanted my father to let me know that he loved me," she shared. "When my boyfriends put their arms around me and say they love me, at least it's *something*. Maybe no one can stop the pain, but at least I forget for a while."

Even the fear that she was pregnant—several times—did not keep Susie from having sex. When one boy abandoned her, she simply went on to the next.

I could see that Susie had a sad future ahead, if she did not change her course. So I helped her understand that the path she had taken would never heal the pain. "You can stop this kind of behavior if you want to," I counseled.

"I could never do it," she cried. "You don't know what I feel inside!"

"What would you do if a boy came up and tried to force you to have sex with him?"

"I'd yell so loudly you'd hear me from here to the next county," Susie answered quickly and proudly. "That'd only be the beginning—I'd kick, claw, and punch until he left me alone."

"Well, it's the same thing here. Once you decide that the short-term gain of having sex is not worth it, you'll fight just as hard to avoid it."

Susie had to understand how her family had influenced her and that she didn't have to look for love in sex before marriage, which would only bring her pain. The pressure to have a boyfriend stemmed from her fear that others might think she couldn't attract anyone. Her imagination concerning what others thought gave her a warped picture of the truth. No one really thought the things she imagined. She had pressured herself into it. Once she understood her mistake, she could learn to love herself enough to say no. She could become an initiator.

Not everyone does drugs or has sex to try to be happy. Bob spent his childhood trying to earn his dad's approval by getting top grades. Because he had to study so hard, he never got the chance to go out for the basketball team or learn to play the trumpet really well. All his efforts went into getting As so that he could hear his dad sing his praises to his friends.

I met Bob when he was twenty-two. He had made it into a fine law school, and though he talked about how proud his dad was of him, Bob appeared depressed. His face had no life in it, and his eyes seemed dull. The very thing he'd done to please his dad had ruined his own feelings about himself.

I showed Bob that he'd actually pressured himself into doing something he hated, because he thought he *had* to have his father's approval. He had never stood his ground with his dad and shared his own desires.

Bob decided to talk to his counselor about changing to another program. Then he would speak to his dad and explain that he had only tried to be a lawyer to please him. I pray his dad understood and loved him as he was.

You need unconditional love—love that supports you when you're in trouble *or* when things are going well. Ideally, you should find that in your home, but not every family has learned the skills that make such love possible.

If your parents can't love you without reservation, tap into some unconditional love in your church, through friends, and perhaps through a counselor who can help heal the hurts. Don't stay out in the cold. Take control of those self-imposed pressures by understanding where you are coming from, how your situation has caused you to move in some poor directions, and how you can change that. Create a step-by-step program for a new life, by turning bad habits into good ones.

As you take charge of life, you'll build your opinion of yourself. Even if you're not facing a real crisis today, you can start by making a few good habits part of your day:

Healthy Self-esteem Habits

These basic steps will help you grow your self-esteem or keep it healthy. Everyone needs them regularly.

> Get plenty of sleep
>> To be at your best each morning
> Eat right
>> So you don't feel grouchy
> Exercise regularly
>> So you look and feel good
> Read God's Word daily
>> To have peace in your life

Once I start forgetting to keep these good habits going, I start forming bad ones—I start to believe I'm not a good speaker, if someone has to call and cancel; if I overhear someone saying something about me, I take it the wrong way. I begin to get so depressed—over nothing!

We all can make a decision to develop self-esteem by thinking thoughts and taking actions that make us positive, happy, whole, and real. Like athletes who spend many hours practicing skills, training, and staying in shape, we have to strengthen our own self-esteem.

We can't do that by putting wrongful pressure upon ourselves and giving up easily when we face the need to change.

What Do I Think Others Think?

Not long ago seventeen-year-old Jim wrote me:

Dear Bill:

I've recently asked Jesus to come into my heart and be my Lord and Savior. I'm really glad you sent me the Bible and daily Bible-study materials to help me grow in his Word.

But there is still pain in my heart. I don't feel great, the way I thought I would once Jesus lived in my heart. I still have a problem. At my school, if you have a girl-friend, you have it made—you can go places and do things with the crowd. I don't have a girlfriend. Though I want one girl to like me, she never looks at me.

What can I do to get her to like me? I've asked her out, but she will not go. At night I cry and get so depressed that I want to die. I know I'm in love with her because I feel so strongly in my heart—I know it's real.

Last year I had a girlfriend and felt wonderful, but she dumped me for another guy. I felt so bad I couldn't believe it; it took me six months to get over her. Now that I'm finally in love with another girl, she will not have a thing to do with me.

Please help me. What should I do?

Jim

When I wrote back to Jim, I pointed out that he was acting as if this girl would take care of all his problems. In his mind, he was trying to live up to the expectations of what people in his school thought. So he thought he could only feel good about himself if a girl had his ring. If he had to walk through the halls alone, he told himself he was insignificant and worthless. Instead of finding other guys who were not dating and joining forces with them, he gave up.

Maybe you've heard the saying, "I'm not who I think I am. I'm not who you think I am. But I am who I think you think I am."

Do you:
- Do what you think you should or what you think others think you should
- Feel good when you do what is right or try to please others, no matter what

- Ask yourself, *Will my friends approve?* before you make a decision
- Wear only clothes that you are sure no one would ever laugh at
- Only wear jewelry others will think is awesome
- Go places you hate because others expect you to go there
- Fear wearing your seat belt, because your friends would think you were weird
- Do less than your best when you study for tests, because you might get better grades than a friend
- Quit a team because one of your friends is kicked off

Don't live up to the expectations of others if those ideas are less than the best for you. Darla had a chance at being first-chair flute in the band, but she gave it up to run away with a friend. When she came back in six months, she couldn't make it in the band again. Regret for that mistake lasts, even though it happened long ago.

A few years after you graduate high school, you probably won't even know the people whose opinions mean so much to you today. Though I graduated with several hundred others, I have only kept in touch with one—my best friend, Steve McKinley—and we only see each other a few times a year.

Today I can't remember the names of the teens who encouraged me to do things I later regretted. I only remember the pain. In college, another student asked if I could take a test for him. At first I said no, but I agreed to do it when he persisted. The professor found us out, and we both got kicked out of the class and received zeros for the entire semester. Not only did it affect my grade-point average, but on my record are the words *Expelled for cheating.* Twenty years later, I can't remember the other boy's name, but I still bear the scars for what I did.

Start to really live today by doing what is right, not what feels good, what everyone else says you should, or what others are doing. Decide for yourself what God says is right and wrong, then do the right.

If everyone else wants to keep on doing wrong, you may not have the power to change that. Just leave. You live in America, a free country. You can go where you want, do what you want, become what you want. All of that starts today.

Are you a girl who will sit through any kind of movie your boyfriend wants to see? Maybe you need to assert your own opinion. I do not take my wife to R-rated movies, because she is too special. You, too, are valuable. Don't treat yourself as if you weren't, and don't let friends or family take advantage of you by leading you into actions that you can't feel proud of. Stand up for yourself firmly but kindly. As they see your strength, others will respect you—even if they give you trouble at first.

Choices for Success or Failure

Do you follow the crowd or do the good, right thing? Will you:
- Avoid negative TV programs
- Say, "I love you," to your parents
- Treat your family with respect
- Sit next to the "class nerd"
- Make others smile on a dark day
- Thank people for the things they've done for you
- Tell a teacher her class was exciting
- Break off bad relationships
- Choose friends who will challenge you to do your best
- Call a friend and thank him for being there for you
- Challenge your classmates to do the right things
- Get into God's Word and pray

Or do you:
- Listen to the most popular radio station—bad message and all
- Avoid your parents as much as you can
- Dump on your brothers and sisters
- Make fun of the kid next to you in homeroom
- Complain that nothing ever goes right for you
- Get into as much trouble as you can with your friends
- Avoid God as much as possible

Living up to the expectations of others, when you know those ideas are wrong or just not right for you, can make you very sorry. If a friend offers advice, listen; think about it; but don't blindly follow. When your dad talks to you about your future, follow his guidance, but make certain he knows what your talents and best attributes are. Decide together if the road he is suggesting is best suited to you.

Do I Have Hope for the Future?

When you look toward the future, what do you expect? How you answer that question will influence how you feel about yourself.

Do you feel:
- Trapped, locked into your past
- Upbeat, knowing you are prepared to do your best in the future
- Doubtful about how you can handle life
- Listless, because you have no goals
- Excited, because you can see where you're going tomorrow
- Sad, since you can see trouble down the road

Sometimes we'll all feel as if we haven't a clue about where to go next. When we face hard times, doubt may drag us down. That's why it's important to have a goal in life. When you have plans and purpose, you'll walk around school with a step that's brisk, with an attitude that says, *I can do this,* and with hope for tomorrow.

People ask me, "What keeps you speaking in schools? Don't you know that half the kids in the seats don't want to be there anyway? Why don't you just throw in the towel?"

"I can't give up," I answer, "because one of those kids is Billy Sanders. He will not listen unless I give every ounce of energy I've got. I have to show him I really love him and that I believe in God, even if his school doesn't want to hear it. Otherwise, I may miss and lose this kid forever. He may never come back." I have hope for the future of each teen I speak to.

I don't want any teen to be like the one I heard about when a classmate wrote me:

> Dear Bill:
>
> The night you spoke to the parents at my school, a boy committed suicide by hanging himself. The sad thing is, he skipped out of school the day you spoke and never heard a word of your assembly. He never heard how you overcame your problems and that he could do it, too.
>
> Bill, I believe that he would be alive today if he had heard you. I'm sorry he wasn't there, but for those who are in your next assembly, never stop saying what you are saying.
>
> With love,
> *Sherry*

I share Sherry's sadness at the loss of that boy, but her letter gives me a picture of just why I speak to teens. When some of them don't listen, I can still put all my love and compassion into reaching out, because I picture that boy who missed my words.

Do you have:
- Things to look forward to
- People's lives to touch
- Goals to reach
- Blessings to impart
- Hope for the future

Without hope, we turn to dope.
Without hope, we sometimes grope.
Without hope, many kids smoke.
Without hope, some kids toke.
Without hope, our lives are choked.

I hope you have hope, but if you don't, you can get it. Don't give up—because then you really have lost out. As long as you're working on building hope, you'll have a chance for a better tomorrow.

3

Improving on What You've Got

By now I hope it's obvious that as flowers, trees, and caterpillars change, so can you. Though the family you were born into, the opinions of others, and your thoughts about yourself and your future may influence you, they don't have to control your life.

God doesn't make losers; he makes choosers. Instead of creating robots, he gave us the ability to decide between right and wrong—to follow God or Satan. We make that decision every day, in large and small places in our lives. Whether it's how to study, who to hang around with, or what to do after school, we'll face rights and wrongs.

Ted knew his dad didn't approve of Jeff, his new friend. To avoid his father's eagle eye, Ted breezed past, while his dad was on the phone.

As he walked to Jeff's house, Ted felt bad. *Dad's just prejudiced,* he rationalized, *because Jeff's brother got in trouble. He doesn't really know Jeff.* So he kept going.

When he got to Jeff's house, James and Gary were already there. "Stick around," Jeff advised. "They usually don't stay long."

The other three went into another room for a while. Ted began to get bored waiting for Jeff, so he opened the bedroom door, to find the three of them smoking marijuana. Before Ted could open his mouth, Jeff's mom drove up.

"Don't let her in. I'll get killed," Jeff told his friend. So Ted went down to talk to her while the other three tried to hide the evidence. The problem was that Mrs. Emerson already had her suspicions. When she entered Jeff's room, she knew what had happened. She called Ted's father, along with the other boys' parents.

Disappointed that his son had ignored his warning about Jeff and that he had sneaked off to meet him and gotten involved in something illegal, Ted's dad came down hard on him. Ted didn't mind the punishment so much, but he did care about the change that occurred in his relationship with his father. "I can't trust you," his dad claimed and for many months would not believe that Ted had given up his friendship with Jeff.

Ted hadn't been using drugs, but he had made a bad choice. For a while, he had to live with that. By learning from his mistake and changing his actions, he finally won his dad's trust again, but he was thankful the consequences hadn't been worse.

Choosing to Change

If you don't like your life, but you keep on doing the same things that have gotten you into trouble, your life will never improve. Had Ted continued his friendship with Jeff, in time he might have begun using drugs—or he might have been caught and prosecuted for drug possession.

Do you know right from wrong? I think so. When you do things in the dark, hide them from others, and tell lies about what you've done, it's wrong.

Change your course by taking three important steps:

1. Identify the wrong in your life.
2. Admit your mistake to yourself and others you have hurt.
3. Develop a new way of life that will correct the wrong.

You see, what you nourish you will encourage. Last year I planted some trees in my yard. Four or five, those nearest my house, got all the water. The three or four in the corner missed out. Today guess which are taller, greener, and healthier? Though I planted them all the same day, the ones I didn't feed had a harder time. Next year I want to try to save the corner trees by taking better care of them.

Feed the good things in your life and replace the bad decisions or situations. Don't fear doing right, because even if someone laughs at you today, you'll still have made a good investment for your future.

If you missed the "watering" of hugs, traditions, and family closeness, you can still choose for the future. Ask God into your life and your heart. Purpose to do what he wants you to do—every day. Slowly but surely you will change for the better.

Making Hard Choices

Changing is rarely easy—but it can become one of the best things in your life. Take out the old, bad habits and replace them with the right ones, and see how your life will improve.

Recently Jane told me she and her boyfriend had been having sex once a week for two years. My talk in her school had convicted her, and she wanted to change, but she feared saying no to him.

"What will he do to me?" she asked. "He told me someday we'll marry. Anyway, I don't think I could live without him."

I pointed out that she was fortunate not to have gotten pregnant or the HIV virus. "You have to put an end to this pain," I advised. "You can't do that without ending the relationship. Though you'll hurt for a while, you will feel better in the end. Look at your future . . . and plan for it."

Jane had to risk the heartache to gain a better tomorrow. Yet it wouldn't come unless she took action that would rid her of the wrongs in her life.

When we plan to do right, we can avoid a lot of pain.

Who has ever:
- Decided on a future as a drug addict
- Wanted to drink and drive and kill an innocent family
- Intended to marry, have four kids, then get a divorce
- Wanted a boyfriend to use her, so she could feel bad
- Intended to get a girl pregnant, so he could know his child was killed through abortion
- Aimed to party, have sex, and get AIDS

No one sets a five-year-plan to do any of these things, yet they happen to people who decide to live life on their own terms, by their own rules, even though they know they're doing wrong. When they have to pay the price of these bad decisions, they often point to God and claim he's unfair, but nothing could be further from the truth. Because he knows the pain in each situation, God has called it wrong. In the Bible, he labels it sin and points out the price that goes with acting this way.

Sin carries pain, scars, and shame, not only for the sinner, but for families, friends, and the world. Dr. Ruth says,"It's no big deal if teens have sex. It's their business, and if they are in love, who does it hurt?" Ask the girl who just found out she's pregnant. Ask the taxpayers who have to pay millions of dollars every day to fund the hospital care for young mothers who can't pay and for deformed babies who never got prenatal care—or the fees of patients at federally funded abortion clinics. Ask the families of those who have contracted AIDS.

Practicing Good Choices

Do you practice sin or right? You make the choice each day.

Are you practicing:
- To become an addict by putting drugs or alcohol in your body
- To be divorced by letting your boyfriends use you
- To have a good family life by learning to love others
- To have a successful career by doing well in school
- For your heavenly future by spending time with God

You see, whatever you do habitually, you practice, and practice doesn't make perfect—it makes permanent.

For a couple of years, I've been on a 3.5 tennis travel team. During my first few matches, I didn't get any better. More matches didn't seem to help. Why? Because I kept making the same mistakes. Once I started taking lessons, I began to improve. Someone had to point out my mistakes, and I had to learn from them.

Does that mean you need a teacher to show you where you've gone wrong? Not necessarily. If you have a serious family problem, you may need an advisor to show you the way out. If a stubborn problem keeps reappearing, you may need to talk to a teacher, parent, or your pastor, but maybe you simply need to identify what you're not proud of and make a change.

Recently I rented the movie *Backdraft,* because I thought it might help my children learn to respect fire. We'd been warned of the sex scenes, so we fast-forwarded over them. I hadn't expected all the profanity, however— and I felt ashamed about letting my children hear it. We talked about this, later, and my son said, "Dad, from now on let's make it a family policy that if we are watching a movie and one bad word comes out, we will shut off the movie and go to another one or play a game instead."

Though I still feel bad about that movie, I'm proud that my son has learned to be a chooser, not a loser. Together we've decided not to have profanity as a part of our lives.

Holding on to Choices

When you choose not to take part in something wrong, people may try to defend it. I challenge people, "Tell me of one person who has had his life enhanced because of alcohol or had better relationships because of drinking a lot." I always get the same answer: "What about people who take NyQuil? Their lives are enhanced." One student tried to tell me about a woman who needed alcohol to get her through depression.

Are these choices improving someone's future? You can get through a cold with other medications. Certainly you can handle depression better if you don't become an alcoholic.

When I met Mary, she told me about her happy family life. Her family was just great, and they got along fine. She had lost her boyfriend, though, and didn't feel like living anymore. Because she felt so down, she decided to seek counseling.

Once Mary started talking to a counselor, it turned out that her boyfriend was just a surface issue. Actually, Mary had never confided in her family. When a problem hit, she handled it herself, exploded, or shared it with her best friend. Once her best friend moved away, in fifth grade, Mary had no one with whom to share her troubles.

In counseling, it came out that Mary had been sexually abused by her baby-sitter's father. When she told her parents, they did not believe her, and she withdrew from them. During her high school years, Mary seriously wanted to commit suicide several times. She confided to her mom that life wasn't worth living and that she wanted to kill herself, but her mom acted as if this happened to everyone. Mary felt as if she'd been slapped in the face for sharing her deepest feelings, so she withdrew even more.

Like every human being, Mary needed to have a relationship with someone; she started to get boyfriends who made her feel important. To keep them, she had to have sex and smoke marijuana with them. Hiding from her pain this way didn't work for long. Each time Mary felt guilty and tried to change things, and the boyfriends would leave.

Deep inside, Mary did want to become close to her parents. With counseling, she has begun to make that happen. She went back to her mom and dad and shared how she felt when they'd ignored her pain. After crying and apologizing, they explained that they had their own troubles at that time and didn't feel they could help her.

Mary has done something about her problem by stopping the negative relationships. Now when she dates, she knows that she has to have limits. Some places and activities are dangerous for her, so she simply won't go to them. She's making right choices.

At first, talking to her parents seemed impossible, but Mary kept on trying. Even when nothing seemed to go smoothly, she kept holding on. Her work has paid off.

Today they live as a real family, sharing their hurts and happiness.

Mary is not the only teen who has lived through pain and rebuilt her life. You can do it, too.

Putting Changes Into Action

Do you need a plan of attack that will help you feel better about yourself, your family, and your future? Begin to turn your life around by asking yourself these questions.

What's My Home Like?

Do you have a good family life that simply needs some fine-tuning? Talk to your parents about how you can make that happen. If you need help, seek out your pastor or a good family friend.

Or maybe you need some counseling because you continually feel sad, hopeless, and hurt. Perhaps you know your family has some serious problems. Don't avoid sharing them with a caring Christian counselor. Step out in faith, no matter what your fears. Help can be found.

Once you start to choose better ways of acting in your family, you'll feel a new sense of direction and accomplishment.

Who Really Loves Me?

God loves you, wants to help you, and will be your best friend. Read your Bible every day to learn how much he cares for you.

1 Corinthians 10:13: "No temptation has seized you except what is common to man. And God is faithful; he will not let you be tempted beyond what you can bear.

But when you are tempted, he will also provide a way out so that you can stand up under it."

Psalm 139:1–4: "O Lord, you have searched me and you know me. You know when I sit and when I rise; you perceive my thoughts from afar. You discern my going out and my lying down; you are familiar with all my ways. Before a word is on my tongue you know it completely, O Lord."

Isaiah 43:2: "When you pass through the waters, I will be with you; and when you pass through the rivers, they will not sweep over you. When you walk through the fire, you will not be burned; the flames will not set you ablaze."

1 Peter 5:7: "Cast all your anxiety on him because he cares for you."

Psalm 62:7, 8: "My salvation and my honor depend on God; he is my mighty rock, my refuge. Trust in him at all times, O people; pour out your hearts to him, for God is our refuge."

Psalm 46:1, 2: "God is our refuge and strength, an ever-present help in trouble. Therefore we will not fear. . . ."

Mary started to believe that when God died, he died for her, and when he rose from the dead, he rose for her. As she went through counseling and read her Bible, she began to see that with him any problem has a solution.

Let God be a part of your healing. Ask him into your life and let him take control, and that change will come.

What Makes Me Happy?

Focus on the good things in your life by writing down five things that make you feel good inside.

Often we worry about or fight for things that do not make us truly happy. For example, did you ever think about all the effort you waste on your clothes? You have to have this outfit, that pair of jeans, or shoes like your best friend's. But I'll bet you didn't put clothes down on your happy list.

Teens with poor self-images often put a lot of importance on their cars, their clothes, being seen with the right friends, and their physical looks. But worrying about all those will never make them happy. When they spend time with the "right" people, dressed in the latest style, they may secretly wish for someone who would like them for themselves. In a crowd, they may feel left out.

What do most teens identify as the things that make them happy? Here they are:

1. Quality time with family. Whether or not he becomes a star, Fred wants Dad to see his games. Jane wants her mom's help making a costume for the class play. To feel loved you have to spend time with your family. Make the effort to be with them.

2. An intimate relationship with their parents. Every teen would like real, unconditional love from Mom and Dad. Young people want intimacy even if they sometimes push their parents away. They want the freedom to talk about anything. They need to be able to say, "I want a hug," and get it.

3. A real friend. Everyone needs at least one close friend. In the movie *Anne of Green Gables,* Anne had moved from an orphanage to the Cuthberts' farm. At her new home, she needed a friend her own age, a "bosom buddy" who would share her thoughts and feelings. When she met Diana and the two girls became fast friends, she filled that need.

Make friends of your own sex—relationships that cannot become clouded by lust and self-gratification. I count myself fortunate to have four or five friends with whom I can talk about anything. Among them, two are special. They never laugh, but treat my confidences with respect.

Don't look for a friend who already has a million others. Chances are that he isn't that close with any of them. Instead find someone who shares your interests and would appreciate your friendship deeply.

4. Feel good about their achievements. Over and over again, I hear about teens' need to feel good about their own achievements and have others praise them. Sure, they need to know about their strong points and do well in some places, but also be aware of the temptation to put too much pressure on themselves to perform.

Pressure Points

Have you ever said to yourself:

If only I could get another A, my teachers would like me

If I could throw two touchdown passes, my dad would be proud of me

If only I had that part in the class play, people would know me

If I get accepted by an Ivy League college, I will have it made

Andy told me how, after every football game, his father would criticize his plays. "You could have thrown the ball a little farther in the first quarter. I don't think you gave it your all," he'd say. Though his dad meant well, to Andy it felt as if he had just been torn down.

My friend Jim Van Dusen's father made it to nearly every baseball, football, and basketball game he played. When Jim came home from a game, his dad would be waiting to tell his son how proud he felt of his game. In his father's mind, Jim was a superstar.

Criticism destroys our ability to feel good about our accomplishments, while support builds us up.

Neither Jim nor Andy went on to play college or professional sports, but because of his father's attitude, Jim has a great relationship with his dad. They can talk and laugh about the good times. Their intimate relationship says, "We'll be friends through this. I'm going to build you up, not tear you down."

Support from your family for your accomplishments is important. Try to build it. Many teens find that, once their parents know they need encouragement, they'll provide it. Still, it may take a while to create that new habit. Work on it together by supporting one another. If you can't seem to get anywhere, seek counseling together.

Choices mean a lot in your life. Whether you're working on a family relationship, deciding on career options, or making a moral determination, look ahead. Ask yourself:

What will happen if I make this choice
How could it affect my future
Will it improve my relationships or damage them
Does God approve of this decision

Positive answers to these will indicate that you are making a good move. With this action, you should improve your life, instead of causing damage.

Remember, you are an improvable model. Good decision making will help you reach important goals in your life. So choose wisely!

PART 2

Building Your House of Self-Esteem

4

Building Blocks of Self-esteem

Since I spend so much time away from my family in order to be with teens, I want to do all I can to understand them. I thought I'd start by looking for information on the teen years of the most famous person of all time—Jesus.

We know plenty about his birth and adult ministry, but despite his fame, only one sentence fully describes Jesus' teen years. Still, that single sentence explains a lot about him. Luke 2:52 says, "And Jesus grew [improved] in *wisdom* and *stature,* and favor with God and men" (italics added).

That line gives us the four areas of our lives on which our self-esteem stands: wisdom, stature, God, and men. It's as if we had a house with a building block at each corner of the foundation—we need all four aligned if we want to have a sturdy structure. A balanced life won't topple over when the winds of trouble blow.

Becoming Wiser Than an Owl

No matter how meager or great they are, we all have some mental capacities. We have the ability to decide if we want to have pizza or a bologna sandwich for lunch; we can opt not to glance at our neighbors' test papers when we don't know an answer; we can choose not to have sex outside of marriage.

Just having the best marks in the class doesn't guarantee you'll make wise choices. Randy forgot that he was having a mid-term math test and went to play basketball with some of his buddies. In class, when the teacher started handing out the papers, he thought, *This will ruin my average. I'll never get into a good college if I blow this test.* In his fear, he decided it wouldn't hurt if he looked over at Brad's answers. *Just to check,* he told himself. *I won't really be cheating.* When he got caught by the teacher, she didn't see it that way. Instead of taking a chance with his own grade, he failed. Now when he applies to college, he has that on his record, along with the poor grade in math. Randy wasn't stupid, but he didn't use wisdom in making what could have been a simple decision.

In ninth grade, Max had some of the highest grades in the school. His future as a lawyer lay before him. Unfortunately two years later the pressure of getting the grades got to him. He started using marijuana, "To help me relax," he told a friend. Soon his grades plummeted because he was so busy "relaxing" that he couldn't bother to do his homework. When colleges saw his downward spiral, they didn't want to touch him. In the end, he felt glad to get into a local community college.

If Randy and Max didn't have what it takes to be wise, what do you need? We'll take a look at that in chapters 5 and 6. You may be surprised at how well you measure up!

Making the Most of Your Body

Stature is another way of saying "physical." When we say that, we think first of our health and athletic abilities. You don't have to be the captain of the football team or the best gymnast in your school to have a body and make the most of it. You can treat yours well or abuse it—that's up to you.

Jaime was one of the most popular kids in school. He did well in all his classes, had a spot on the baseball team, and never lacked for girlfriends. He loved to party with his friends. At first he only held a drink to look like part of the crowd; then he started sipping the beer and decided it didn't taste too bad. Soon he began drinking every weekend. His girlfriends began to slip away when they saw that he only wanted booze. Then his mother faced him with the problem: "You know that being an alcoholic doesn't necessarily mean you drink all the time. Binge drinkers get drunk once in a while, but they are still addicted."

At first Jaime didn't want to believe he had a problem, but when he tried not to drink, he craved it. *Why did I do this to my body?* he asked. Fortunately, he has made great strides in overcoming his addiction. "But it hurts," he says, "to know that I could have avoided this if I'd made some wise decisions about going to a few parties."

Treat yourself well. Exercise regularly. Eat good food—not junk food all the time. Don't put drugs or alcohol in your body, and don't let a cigarette touch your lips. In the long run, you'll thank yourself.

Physical traits also include your talents and abilities. Do you like to work with your hands? Do crafts? Use your brain to figure out difficult problems? Because they require your body, these all have to do with your stature.

Anything you do with your body is a learned skill, and skills are important to self-image, because through them people accomplish goals, do something for others, and display themselves. Skill comes with effort. For example, you can't learn to rebuild a car engine by sitting in the waiting room and watching a mechanic. You have to stand right next to him, and he has to show you each step. Then you have to take the tools in your hands and try for yourself before you will get the hang of it. Only with many hours' practice will you be able to do the job smoothly and quickly. Then at the end of your training, you will take pride in your accomplishments. You will feel that you can do something for the person whose car breaks down, and that will give you a sense of importance to others.

Everyone has some physical talents to develop. Make the most of yours, and you'll see yourself in a new light.

Stature also speaks of how others see you. Do your actions make them look up to you, admire you for your willingness to take a stand, or come to you for encouragement? All these are signs of a good reputation.

When you habitually make poor choices, create trouble in relationships, or complain endlessly, you earn a negative reputation.

Whether you have earned yourself a bad reputation or gotten it through a few unkind remarks of others, you can change what you have today. Chapter 10 will discuss a few simple steps that will get you started on a new you!

Soul Truths

"God doesn't really exist," Polly told her sister. "If he did, why would he let all these bad things go on in the world?"

Anna felt awful that her sister hadn't appreciated the changes in her own life enough to believe in Jesus too. Still, she held her ground by pointing out all the good things God gave people. "It's people who make the mistakes, Polly. Don't blame God."

Polly didn't seem impressed by the argument, but when her best friend, Cindy, had an accident, she sought out Anna. "Pray for Cindy," she asked. "The doctors say her broken leg may not heal right. It could leave her with a limp. That would mean she couldn't be on the track team ever again."

Lots of people act as if God doesn't exist—until they need a favor from him. Do you:

- Treat him as a celestial Santa, whose job it is to rain down gifts when you're in trouble
- Spend time daily getting close to God, seeking his will, and trying to live by his Word, the Bible
- Pretend he doesn't exist, because you're afraid he'd ask too much of you
- Feel as if no one else cares, so why should God

Either looking on God as an endlessly benevolent gift giver or as a meanie who lives in the sky shows that your spiritual corner could use some improvement. Who could respect a God who let himself be endlessly used, with never an objection? As for the meanie God, no wonder you don't want to spend much time with one who only wants to cause you grief! If you see him that way, no one can blame you for trying to shut him out. However, neither of these views accurately describes Jesus. He is balanced. He doesn't accept all you do as being right. Instead, he shows you your wrongdoing and gives you a new start.

Meanness is not part of God's plan. Though you may feel pain when life becomes difficult, he stays at your side, helps you through it, and brings you to a better place. As you obey him, your life improves.

Today start believing in him and walking close to him, and you will have a strong spiritual base to work from.

Getting a Better Social Life

When the Bible talks about Jesus finding favor with man, it's talking about his social life. Humans all need to get along with other people.

How we deal with others has a lot to do with what we learned at home.

Did your family treat you:
- As if you were special and loved for yourself
- As if no one were better looking than you—but lots of people were brighter
- As if you deserved to be hit, yelled at, and complained about
- As if you always had to earn love by doing the right thing

That will influence how you expect others to treat you and how you feel about yourself.

Were your parents:
- Always so busy being your best friends that they could never tell you you'd done something wrong
- Frequently critical of anything you did
- Supportive and understanding when you had trouble, but willing to teach you right from wrong
- Distant and cold—acting as if you were in the way all the time

Does your family treat others as if:
- They were important and needed to be treated well
- Everyone was out to get your family

- They needed to be ignored, because they always caused trouble
- No one in your family could be as important as friends, colleagues, or acquaintances

That attitude probably describes how you see friends, distant relations, or strangers.

How your family taught you to treat others will have a great impact on your social life. If they had many friends, you may, too. If they treated people as if they were dangerous, you may not trust others. You don't have to remain in the pattern of your family, though, if it was not positive. Instead attempt to step out on your own:

If your family never got close to others, make a point of spending time getting to know a few friends well instead of avoiding people or having such a busy life that you never get close to anyone. Learn people skills through a pastor, youth leader, or friend who knows how to have close friendships.

If your family had too many friends, focus on the one or two you like best, and deepen relationships.

Build trust by looking at your expectations for others and proving them wrong, if you grew up in a family that believed others only hurt you. Look at the people you know who have tried to help you, shown that they cared, and been turned away. How could they help you, when you didn't let them? Can you turn them into friends by giving them a chance?

Look at how you have carried messages from your family life into your social contacts. When you discover a negative message, work up a plan to change your natural reaction by challenging your thoughts, taking a new view of the situation, and trying another plan of action.

Chapter 15 will give you some communication tips that will help you make some of these changes.

In the following chapters, we'll talk more about how these building blocks influence us and how we can improve them. There are some steps you can take to begin overcoming your weak spots and strengthening your strong ones.

5

Me, Wise?
I'm Too Dumb!

Do you need to have the IQ of Albert Einstein to have wisdom? Not according to the Bible. Over and over God tells us to value wisdom, but he never even mentions our smarts.

Psalm 90:12: "Teach us to number our days aright, that we may gain a heart of wisdom."

Romans 16:19: ". . . I want you to be wise about what is good. . . ."

Ephesians 5:15, 16: "Be very careful, then, how you live—not as unwise but as wise, making the most of every opportunity, because the days are evil."

James 3:13: "Who is wise and understanding among you? Let him show it by his good life, by deeds done in the humility that comes from wisdom."

From these verses, you can see that wisdom involves what you do, how you decide to act, more than it does what kind of grades you get or how many talents you have. Making good choices will show the wisdom that is inside you.

A high IQ may not come with wisdom. Why? Because being smart and wise aren't the same. King Solomon realized that when God came to him and said, "Ask for whatever you want me to give you." Solomon could have had nations to conquer, enough money for the biggest and best chariot, or friends who would never leave him. What did Israel's leader ask for? Wisdom. "Give your servant a discerning heart," he asked, "to govern your people and to distinguish between right and wrong. For who is able to govern this great people of yours?" (1 Kings 3:5, 9).

Solomon would become the wisest king Israel ever had. He discovered the true mother of a child by ordering the two women who fought over him to split the child in half. The one who willingly gave up her child, so he could live, was the mother. That kind of wisdom made him famous. Unfortunately, it only lasted as long as Solomon stayed close to God. Later on, he fell into sin and made many unwise decisions that broke up his kingdom after his death.

You may never need to settle a legal battle, like Solomon, but you must make wise decisions in your own life. I want you to be able to spot trouble before you invite it into your home or pick out good ideas from bad ones. You don't have to be a king to want that!

What Wisdom Takes

You may be wiser than you already know. Take "The Wisdom Quiz" on page 59 and find out how you rate.

The Wisdom Quiz

__ 1. I am gentle and kind to other people.

__ 2. I make fun of other people when they don't do things the way I do them.

__ 3. I study as hard as I can, even if I don't get straight As.

__ 4. I figure that an hour is enough to study every day.

__ 5. Even when people are different from me, I treat them with respect.

__ 6. People who don't agree with me are wrong. What does it matter if I tell them so?

__ 7. When I see a movie that has profanity in it, I turn it off.

__ 8. What's wrong with a good dirty joke? It doesn't hurt anyone.

__ 9. Even though I could get away with drinking, I have better ways to spend my Saturday nights.

__ 10. What fun is a weekend if you can't party? No one gets hurt, so what does it matter?

__ 11. When a friend asks me where I've been, I tell the truth, even if it means we'll disagree.

__ 12. My parents don't need to know where I am all the time. If it's none of their business, I tell them what they want to hear.

__ 13. When I go to work, I do my best, even if it's not always right.

__ 14. I quit my job because I didn't like the way the boss ran things.

__ 15. Sure I make mistakes, but so does everyone. Losers are people who give up.

__ 16. When I'm wrong, I try not to admit it. After all, why should I invite criticism?

Give yourself one point for every odd-numbered answer you had. Now score your answers.

0–3: You haven't spent much time trying to be wise. Read carefully to discover how you can improve your wisdom quotient.

4–6: You know what's wise and what isn't. Now's the time to improve your understanding and put these truths into your life.

7–8: You need to share your knowledge about wisdom with others. Just be sure you do it in a wise and gentle way.

I know what it's like to be not so wise. I drank and used drugs during college—and now I can't have my own children (ours are adopted). I lied to my parents when they smelled the marijuana in our house. Many times I drove while I was drunk and endangered the lives of others.

After I married, I lied to my wife. To this day, I regret that mistake, but I can't change it.

None of those were wise choices.

I learned that I didn't have to stay unwise. On Christmas Day, 1978, I made my life's wisest decision when I asked Jesus to take away my sins and live in me. Now I know what it's like to be God's child. He's always there for me and has given me eternal life.

Two years later I went back to college and finished up the ten credit hours I needed to graduate. Though it took some hard work, it was a wise decision.

Like a muscle, you need to exercise wisdom to make it stronger. You can start by taking these simple steps:

1. Read and memorize God's Word. I started getting wise when I asked Jesus to change my life, but it didn't stop there. I had to keep on growing in him by learning about him through the Bible. Knowing God and getting closer to him will give you deeper wisdom. You'll avoid many mistakes by knowing how to live well. The Bible's principles will pass the test of time.

When I memorize the Scriptures, I have wonderful things happen to me. Peace fills my heart. On the other hand, when I forget or avoid God's Word, things get me upset and angry.

2. *Trust God.* Now that you know what he says, believe he will do it. Know that he has your best interests at heart and gives you guidelines so that you can have only the best in life. Please learn to trust him.

3. *Trust your parents.* Most parents have their child's best interests at heart. Ask yours for advice. Talk to them on an intimate level that says, "I want to be friends with you."

4. *Have the right heroes.* Look at how others have acted. When a friend of mine was growing up, his mother told him that, if he wanted to be wise, he would have to spend time with wise people. If he wanted to earn money, he would have to walk with people who had done that. What kind of heroes do you have?

I challenge students all over the country to look for heroes with inside stuff. What they look like on the outside doesn't matter. I look up to Michael Jordan because of his inside stuff, more than the wonders he does on the basketball court. Michael will not advertise tobacco or alcohol, because he wants to be a real hero for kids.

Have some local heroes, too. Anthony Iannacone made the *New York Times* for cleaning up his neighborhood. He doesn't stop crime—he blots out graffiti on Sullivan Street, in New York City, shovels snow, and provides the trees with more dirt when they need it. Why? "Because I like to live nice," he reported.

However, a hero doesn't need to make the papers. Do you admire your grandfather for his honesty, simplicity, and love of nature? Or maybe your homeroom teacher makes you feel proud because she cares for kids, spends time with them when they hurt, and gets them the help they need.

5. *Keep two lists.* One list will describe the things you need to improve on and the other the wise things you have done. Work on the parts that need improvement and encourage yourself by looking at your wise choices.

When you live wisely, you feel better about yourself. Suddenly you have a clear direction to travel in. You avoid the roadblocks of bad decision making and have more peace in your life. It's worth it, isn't it?

6

What Fills My Mental Bucket?

We can reprogram our minds with wisdom, but what if the old attitudes and messages keep getting in the way?

Nancy knew that God loved her, but her father had deserted her mother when she was only a baby. Though her father's parents stood by her and her mother, she had a hard time believing in the words she read in her Bible. Sure it said God would never desert her, but how could she know that? After all, he let her father walk out on Mom.

Nancy sees God through her past experience. It's as if she had a bucket filled with the past wrongs inflicted upon her and her family, and she has a hard time emptying that bucket.

She is not alone. Each of us has a bucket. Ideally our parents filled it with kind words, lots of hugs, and actions that showed their love. That's the way God intended it to be. As we grew, they should have modeled loving actions day in and day out, so we would know what God is like.

Lots of people didn't have that in their families. Mom and Dad may have been too preoccupied, confused, or struggling with an addiction. So the view we got of God reflects our view of our parents.

Maybe it isn't your view of God that was influenced. Perhaps your parents spent all their time at home and never had many friends. Now you want to reach out to other people, but you feel as if you can't trust them. Even though your parents never told you not to trust people, they acted it out. You find it hard to open up to others.

What's in your mental pail today? Examine your thoughts and attitudes to see where there is garbage in your pail. Then look at the good things you've filled it up with.

Mental Review

What makes you feel negative, uncared for, and sad?
In your family:

In your community:

At school:

What makes you feel important, needed, and wanted?
In your family:

In your community:

At school:

I listed my wife as one of the things that made me feel good, because she can even disagree with me and make me feel loved. Three of my best friends made the list, because they listen to my confidences and don't spread them around. Who are the special people in your life who have made you feel good, achieve more, and go farther? What activities made you feel good about yourself? I feel good about the books I have written.

As you list these things, remember that God doesn't value you for the number of goals you make, how many friends you have, or how together your family life is. You don't have to be perfect to feel good about yourself. Though it's great to have high standards, things that make you feel good don't have to be earth shattering. Helping your younger brother finish a model airplane or teaching your sister how to cook may have made you feel needed. That counts as much as running an election campaign for your class president.

Some things on your list may make you feel good for a while, but in the long run you'll regret them. Sandy told me a familiar story when she said that the only love she knew was what she got from her boyfriend. If she stopped having sex, she knew he'd leave her. She couldn't bear the pain, so she wouldn't give up the dangers of sex. In the long run, she may have the hurt of AIDS, pregnancy, or a failed marriage to add to her current pain. Yet she won't give him up. I hope she learns to solve her problems instead of hiding from them. In the end, she may pay a deadly price for her "love" today.

What makes you feel good today and has dangerous consequences? Is it a relationship on the road to nowhere, an attitude that hurts others and yourself, or a thrill that will only lead to death? Don't let your emotional hurts or your memories keep you from the best.

Changing Thoughts

We've spent a lot of time looking at the things that influence us. Why? So we can understand why we think the way we do. Once we understand the relationship between thinking, feeling, and actions, we can begin to clear out the mental garbage in our buckets and fill them with something good.

Thoughts and emotions. How we feel and how we think have a lot to do with each other. Lots of times we focus so much on how we feel that we don't realize how much control our thoughts have over our emotions.

For example, on your way to school, suppose you walk past a crowd of teens, and some of them start to laugh. You look up, and it seems as if they're laughing at you. As you head toward your first class, you feel worthless because you're sure they thought you were funny looking. Didn't one of them tell you he didn't like your shirt the other day? You go into your classroom, and one of the group is telling about a funny story he heard on the way to school. All of a sudden you know you weren't the reason they laughed—and you feel as if you're on the top of the world again.

When we think good thoughts about ourselves, we're more likely to feel good about ourselves. When we think we're worthless, that's the way we'll feel, too.

Just as you didn't have to accept the message that you were no good from those teens, you don't have to believe all the put-downs you've gotten at home or in school. Learn to identify the truth of the situation, instead. Did a teacher criticize you because he was jealous of your accomplishments, not because you were wrong? Was your dad hard on you because he had trouble at work?

Challenge thoughts. Lots of times you assume things are true when they aren't. When you start to feel a familiar negative emotion, identify why you feel that way. Did your teacher's criticism remind you of a complaint your mother always has about a neighbor? Did a friend say innocent words that reminded you of how your sister makes fun of you? You may be following along with a familiar thought that isn't true at all. Stop in your tracks before you react to a situation that isn't real. Reevaluate where you are now.

Argue with yourself. When you find a negative thought in your mind, stop and argue with it. If someone laughs at you on your way to school, don't borrow trouble. Realize that it's not your problem if she's being mean behind your back, and decide not to let yourself feel down.

When Nancy realized that she had trouble believing that God would not desert her, she challenged that thought. After all, God was much greater than her earthly father. He had never given her reason to think he would desert her. Nancy began reading the Bible's promises and studying how God was a Father to her. When she began to feel abandoned by her dad, Nancy told God about it and remembered the verses she had studied.

"Some days I still feel bad, but I'm beginning to have more faith," she told me. "Once I realized how different my dad and God are, I could see that I didn't have much to fear."

Don't let fear or doubt stay in your mind without confronting it. Overcoming negative thoughts may take time and patience, but you can slowly change your habits to more positive ones.

7

How Does My Stature Measure Up?

The Bible says Jesus grew in stature. When I looked up that word in the dictionary, it said, "Natural height." Whether he was short or tall, I don't think that's all Luke 2:52 is talking about.

The dictionary also defined *stature* as "quality or status." When people looked at Jesus, they could see the quality of his life. From what they saw, they developed an opinion of him—he had stature.

Notice that he didn't have stature naturally—he grew. He achieved more and moved forward.

Three ingredients make up our stature: our looks, talents, and reputation. Let's take a look at each, so we can develop some tools for increasing our stature with people and God.

Outside Stature

Looks are the first things people notice about you—and like it or not, people make decisions based on what they see.

The other day my family and I went to a mall, where I saw a seventeen-year-old boy whose appearance announced just how he felt about himself. For several days he hadn't washed his hair. He was dressed in a black leather jacket that read, *Sex, Drugs and Rock n Roll,* with a big X through the word *drugs;* black jeans and black boots completed his outfit. One wrist sported a tattoo. From his fingers hung a cigarette that he puffed on as he consumed a healthy lunch of Mountain Dew and a bag of chips.

At his side an even grubbier friend exchanged profanity with him. I felt embarrassed that my children had to hear that.

I know these boys were looking for attention with the way they dressed. Maybe their families don't reach out to them, and they need someone to talk to them, care, and tell them they are loved. I hurt for them, but the path they are taking will only bring them disappointment.

The physical area is often the easiest one in which to make improvements. You can choose to be clean, get exercise, and wear neat clothing. Using deodorant, brushing your teeth, and taking a shower are pretty simple chores.

Recently a boy walked up to me in a school and asked why other teens made fun of him. Though he was only in the ninth grade, he was about six feet tall. Kids tripped him in the hall and made fun of him. No one could change his height, but he could get a haircut, keep clean, and begin to shave. A few simple changes could make a big difference.

Do you need to lose weight? If you simply have to exercise more or eat less, make the effort to start a simple program. Keep going by encouraging yourself with your progress and looking toward your long-term goal.

For some, weight is a way of dealing with a bigger problem. If a family has sexual abuse in it, a girl may gain weight to make herself unattractive to men. Once she can honestly face her pain, she may be able to lose the pounds.

Others have such a poor self-image that they won't eat, or they eat and vomit up the food. For these girls, too, counseling may help by confronting the problems that have caused the physical trouble.

We all need to be careful that we don't put food that undermines our self-image into our bodies. Whether we eat to fill an emotional need or consume enough fast foods to harm our bodies for a lifetime, we need to see that eating will influence how we feel. Plenty of sweets may make you feel good for a short time, but when your blood-sugar level plummets a few hours later, you'll probably feel down—and hungry again. Put the best into your body!

Things You Do

With your body you can do lots of things—jump, sing, write, think, and talk. You have a thousand fun and wonderful talents. Some people love to sing, while others barely croak out a tune. Math whizzes often don't like to study English, and people who like English frequently dread algebra class. It's not that one is wrong and the other right—it's just that people are usually gifted in one area and not another.

God has made you special by giving you gifts and talents in your own unique package. It's as if you had a gift to unwrap—you have to find which abilities are inside and make the most of them.

Find out what he's given you by searching it out. When you don't like math, you still have to go to geometry class, but you don't have to become a mathematician. Look for the things you do enjoy. Try out a lot of different areas and discover what's hidden in your special package by studying a new subject, starting a new hobby, or going new places.

Though you might not expect it, when you can accomplish some goals and try some new things, you'll start to feel good about yourself. Confidence comes when you try a new challenge, practice it, and do well at it. Then if you help someone else with your new talent, your self-esteem grows. Each of us naturally has the desire to help someone out.

Think about it. If someone else asks your opinion, don't you feel important? If you can give a friend a hand, don't you feel good? It's built into us to want to help others, and we feel good when we can do that. So we need to identify the ways we can help others and put them to use.

Develop your talents—for your sake and the sake of others.

In Chapter 9 we'll look at some ways you can discover what you are really good at and how you can develop the best God has for you. Based on what you learn about yourself, you can develop some goals for your future and find joy in the present.

How People See You

Jesus grew in stature in the minds of others. Many thought well of him, because they knew the kinds of things he did.

Though you may try to avoid the opinions of others, you will get some ideas about how they think of you. If you hear you're the best student in the class, you'll feel good about yourself—you may even get a swelled head. On the other hand, if parents and teachers always complain about your grades, you won't feel too great. Everyone naturally earns a reputation for what he or she is good or bad at.

Sometimes old reputations hold onto you. I met with a boy who felt depressed because nothing ever seemed to work out for him. It turned out that he had been nicknamed *Turtle Legs,* when he was a child, because he was a slow-moving toddler. Unfortunately, the name stuck long after he had grown up. For many years, he held on to that image of himself as being slow and didn't put effort into his schoolwork or other areas of life.

Don't let an old reputation bring you down. Instead seek to build one for honesty, fairness, kindness, and doing the best you can.

Most of all, accept yourself as someone who deserves a good reputation. To a friend, Marie complained that she was worthless—a big, fat zero. Now that was not true, but to Marie it seemed so very real. She's made it true in her own mind.

Marie's friend helped her look at her talents. "You are a wonderful baby-sitter and a great encourager," she pointed out. "Use your gift of encouragement to write letters to friends, neighbors, and other people in the community."

Marie did that. When the people she wrote to shared how much her letters meant, she got a reputation that matched her personality. Parents began to ask her to baby-sit even more, and she's become vibrant and hopeful. Discovering her natural talents changed her life and brought her the reputation she wanted all along.

Have you made unwise decisions? Do you have a reputation as a disaster? You don't have to keep it. Develop your positive side, and soon you'll earn a new, happier image.

In the next three chapters, we'll take a look at the ways your physical side influences your self-esteem and how you can make changes. Sure, some things, like the texture of your hair, the size of your nose, or your height, can't be altered. Maybe you will never do well in science or write the great American novel. Nonetheless, you do have some physical gifts that can build your self-esteem—gifts that are just for you, suited to your own size and style. Making the most of them is a challenge and a joy. Together we'll scope them out.

8

Looking at Myself from the Inside Out

When you look at your stature, what do you focus on? Do you have to make the yearbook as half of the best-looking couple? Do you need to have huge muscles to attract a date for the prom?

If so, take a new look at physical appearances—from Jesus' point of view.

How Handsome Was Jesus?

When we think of the physical, we often think of our bodies—and to most people, that means "beautiful." So many teens feel as if being handsome would solve all their problems or being beautiful would make their phones ring. If that were true, why do beautiful people take their lives every year? Why do they ruin themselves with drugs and alcohol? Why do they give sex for "love" that doesn't last?

Jesus had crowds follow him. Almost a dozen close friends were willing to die for his message. Yet he wasn't beautiful.

Isaiah 53:2, 3 (TLB): "In God's eyes he was like a tender green shoot, sprouting from a root in dry and sterile ground. But in our eyes there was no attractiveness at all, nothing to make us want him. We despised him and rejected him—a man of sorrows, acquainted with bitterest grief. We turned our backs on him and looked the other way when he went by. He was despised and we didn't care."

Nothing in Jesus' physical appearance drew those crowds. He was not handsome. But he brought healing to lives, hope to the hopeless, and love to those who felt empty. For that, people followed him.

That doesn't mean you should ignore how you or others look. We can't help making some decisions about people by their looks, but we also need to peer inside, to see what goes on underneath.

Steve looked so good to Amy. He was handsome, drove a sporty car, took her to all the exciting places in town, and spent time on the phone with her. At first she felt like a princess, because he treated her so well. Then after a while, she realized that Steve was changing. He started "going out with the boys" and insisting that where he went was his private business.

Later a girl from another school asked if Amy and Steve had broken up, and Amy found out that all the "nights with the boys" had been dates with another girl. He had lied to the other girl, too.

"If he only wanted to date once in a while, I could have handled that," she told her mom. "I don't own him. But I broke up with him because he lied to me. When I asked him about it, it didn't seem to matter to him. 'What's the big deal? It was only a little white lie.' But he also lies to his family, and yesterday I heard him lying to a teacher. Where would it end?"

Amy looked inside Steve and didn't much like what she saw. The attractive body and fun times couldn't change his dishonesty.

Do you care about the not-so-beautiful person who is kind and hard working, or do you only look on the outside?

Jesus cared for the beautiful people and the nerds and low-lives. Perhaps he could do that because he knew what it meant to be despised by others. He knew what it meant to be unpopular with the "right people" of his day—the Pharisees.

Matthew 9:9–13 (TLB): "As Jesus was going down the road, he saw a tax collector, Matthew, sitting at a tax collection booth. 'Come and be my disciple,' Jesus said to him, and Matthew jumped up and went along with him. Later, as Jesus and his disciples were eating dinner [at Matthew's house] there were many notorious swindlers there as guests!

"The Pharisees were indignant. 'Why does your teacher associate with men like that?'

"'Because people who are well don't need a doctor! It's the sick people who do!' was Jesus' reply. Then he added. 'Now go away and learn the meaning of this verse of Scripture, "It isn't your sacrifices and your gifts I want—I want you to be merciful." For I have come to urge sinners, not the self-righteous, back to God.'"

The Pharisees did everything for looks, but underneath all their fine clothes and good deeds that everyone could see was a bad attitude. Jesus saw right through them—and they didn't like that.

When you ask Jesus to forgive you for your sins, the humility that follows should help you look inside others, too. If they are caring and kind, if they put others first and reach out to the hurting, they have real stature—the kind Jesus wants us to have.

Real Attractiveness

What a person is on the inside is far more real than any outward appearance, because the one who looks so good can be deceiving. Have you ever been taken advantage of by someone who was beautiful, but only wanted something from you? Have you ever seen a second-hand-car ad that made the vehicle look good—until the warranty expired, and you had to fix the engine? How about the person who quotes the Bible—and then steals all the church's money? Even the people who look the best can be the most deceiving.

> *2 Corinthians 11:14, 15 (TLB):* "Yet I am not surprised! Satan can change himself into an angel of light, so it is no wonder his servants can do it too, and seem like godly ministers. In the end they will get every bit of punishment their wicked deeds deserve."

Real attractiveness means you look good on the inside and feel good about who you are. Remember God's definition of self-esteem: Your uniqueness (your inside stuff) + your relationship with him.

How can you spot the really attractive person? The Bible tells us, "Kindness makes a man attractive. And it is better to be poor than dishonest" (Prov. 19:22 TLB). Look for the person who is caring, gentle, trustworthy, and reliable. Those inside qualities last, when looks and material possessions have disappeared.

I can't help thinking that the divorce statistics hang around the 50 percent mark because so many people only look at the outside. They don't seek the truth about each other—about problems, pains, and secrets that hold them back. If their marriage doesn't work, they figure they will simply try again. But God says marriage lasts forever, and what he puts together no one should part.

More Than How You Look

If you only think about what you look like on the outside, you will always feel nervous when you give a speech. *Do they like me? Do I look good?* you'll wonder. As you talk to friends, you'll have a performance mentality—you'll feel as if you were always on stage and not quite good enough. Why does this happen? Because you're focusing on the outside, not the qualities that will really attract people. You can't have real appeal or change the world with your face. You need to have inner qualities.

Remember the world's and Satan's view of self-esteem: What you do and look like from the outside + How others accept you, praise you, need you, and love you. When you follow along with that view, the world and circumstances—not you—control how you feel.

Inside Attractions

Rate yourself on each of these qualities, from 1 to 5 (1 means you need a lot of work in this, while 5 means you've pretty much got it under control).

__ I am always loyal to my friends, even if it means confronting them when they've done something wrong.

__ When I take on a project, I do it diligently, even if I find it tough.

__ If someone tells me something in confidence, I keep that secret, even when it's hard.

__ Instead of listening to gossip, I learn about people from their actions.

__ When a friend looks good in front of others, I feel happy. I don't get jealous or angry.

__ Even when I don't have to, I do nice things for my family. Other people don't have to know about it for me to feel good inside.

__ I enjoy buying my friends and family small gifts, even when there is no special occasion to celebrate. They deserve my best all the time.

__ When I know someone's in need, I try to pitch in. Buying groceries for a needy family, helping out at the church picnic, or visiting a friend in the hospital would make me happy.

How did you score in each area? Do you see places that need work? I hope you have more attractions inside than outside. You see, you can't be happy when you only view your physical looks, because with them you can't do much for others. With your talents and gifts, you can touch others' lives.

Body Life

God doesn't say our bodies aren't important. He gave them life, so he knows their worth. He wants us to value them the way he does. That's why he gave us twelve commands about them.

1. Give yourself completely to God. Serving God does not mean just asking him into your heart. To live for him, you have to use your hands, your mind, and your feet. It takes everything you've got to make him Lord of your life.

Romans 6:13, 14 (TLB): "Do not let any part of your bodies become tools of wickedness, to be used for sinning; but give yourselves completely to God—every part of you—for you are back from death and you want to be tools in the hands of God, to be used for his good purposes. Sin need never again be your master, for now you are no longer tied to the law where sin enslaves you, but you are free under God's favor and mercy."

You can't let your body sin and stay close to God. When you disobey him, sin controls you. Yield to the

Lord today, and he will give you the power to overcome that sin. Freedom lies only in him.

2. Make your body a living sacrifice. You don't have to die to serve Jesus. God wants a living sacrifice who can show people how knowing him makes a difference in life.

> *Romans 12:1, 2 (TLB):* "And so, dear brothers, I plead with you to give your bodies to God. Let them be a living sacrifice, holy—the kind he can accept. When you think of what he has done for you, is this too much to ask? Don't copy the behavior and customs of this world, but be a new and different person with a fresh newness in all you do and think. Then you will learn from your own experience how his ways will really satisfy you."

When people see the way you live, let them realize you have offered yourself up to God. Let them know that you do the right things because Jesus Christ is your Savior and that you would rather please him than people.

3. Make your body a holy place. Be careful about the things that go into and come out of your body.

> *1 Corinthians 3:17 (TLB):* "If anyone defiles and spoils God's home, God will destroy him. For God's home is holy and clean, and you are that home."

Every time you use drugs, alcohol, or even profanity, they destroy God's home, your body. Be sure that you keep your temple as holy as possible. Remember, the Lord lives there. Just as you wouldn't want to offer him a dirty room if he stayed overnight at your house, don't give him a filthy place in which to park his Spirit.

4. Let your body prepare you for your heavenly home. You know this body won't live forever, so keep in mind how it will influence what you do for eternity.

1 Peter 2:11, 12 (TLB): "Dear brothers, you are only visitors here. Since your real home is in heaven I beg you to keep away from the evil pleasures of this world; they are not for you, for they fight against your very souls.

"Be careful how you behave among your unsaved neighbors; for then, even if they are suspicious of you and talk against you, they will end up praising God for your good works when Christ returns."

If you walk the way the world does, you can't be a shining light for God. However, you can make a difference if you live so that he will be pleased by your actions.

5. Be a light in a dark world. Don't doubt it; it's a dark world out there. You see the sin all around you. When people sin, they do not feel happy—at least not for long. Bring hope into their lives by showing them that people can live for good, do the right things, and enjoy life.

Matthew 5:13–16 (TLB): "You are the world's seasoning, to make it tolerable. If you lose your flavor, what will happen to the world? And you yourselves will be thrown out and trampled underfoot as worthless. You are the world's light—a city on a hill, glowing in the dark for all to see. Don't hide your light! Let it shine for all; let your good deeds glow for all to see, so that they will praise your heavenly Father."

Shining for Jesus may not always be easy, but it is valuable. Don't let the darkness of the world infiltrate you. Shine in his Holy Spirit power.

6. Purpose your body to be dead to sin. How you see the change in yourself will have a lot to do with how you act. If you decide, *I can't give this up,* you won't. On the other hand, if you decide that sin isn't worth it, you'll be able to hang in there—with God's help.

Romans 6:11 (TLB): "So look upon your old sin nature as dead and unresponsive to sin. . . ."

Sin doesn't need to live in you any longer. When Christ died and defeated sin by rising from the dead on the third day, you died to sin.

7. Listen when God speaks. Don't wait to hear a voice from the clouds, telling you what to do. Instead Jesus speaks softly to a listening heart. Be waiting for his direction.

Romans 6:11 (TLB): ". . . Be alive to God, alert to him, through Jesus Christ our Lord."

You may hear his direction through *other people, his Word,* or *your heart.* Tune in to him by fellowshipping with him day by day—spending time reading the Bible, praying, and worshiping with his people. If you do that, you will hear him when he whispers, instead of only when he shouts. Make Jesus your best friend by sharing your life with him. You talk to your friends, don't you? He's just waiting to tell you something today.

8. Refuse to let sin master you. Just because you know Jesus, don't believe you will never feel any temptation. Satan will want to stop you, but now that you know God, you can say no to the things that are wrong.

Romans 6:12 (TLB): "Do not let sin control your puny body any longer; do not give in to its sinful desires."

Your body may be puny, but through Jesus you can avoid doing and saying things that hurt, thinking thoughts that do not honor God, and living in a way that hurts you and others. Imagine, no matter how short and skinny you might be, in Jesus you are powerful!

9. Let the Holy Spirit have power over your body. You can't do it alone. Satan will fool you every time if you resist him in your own strength. But the devil can't win over God.

> *Romans 8:12–14 (TLB):* "So dear brothers, you have no obligations whatever to your old sinful nature to do what it begs you to do. For if you keep on following it you are lost and will perish, but if through the power of the Holy Spirit you crush it and its evil deeds, you shall live. For all who are led by the Spirit of God are sons of God."

As you resist the tricks and temptations of Satan and work for the Spirit, you and others will know that you are a child of God. With the Holy Spirit at work in you, you are a winner!

10. Don't ever harm your body. God lives in your body and gave his Son for you. No longer can you say that you only harm yourself when you abuse your body.

> *1 Corinthians 6:19, 20 (TLB):* "Haven't you yet learned that your body is the home of the Holy Spirit God gave you, and that he lives within you? Your own body does not belong to you. For God has bought you with a great price. So use every part of your body to give glory back to God, because he owns it."

Let your body become a residence God can be proud of.

11. Keep your body in control. How you live physically shows a lot about your spiritual life.

> *1 Corinthians 9:27 (TLB):* "Like an athlete I punish my body, treating it roughly, training it to do what it should, not what it wants to. Otherwise I fear that after enlisting others for the race, I myself might be declared unfit and ordered to stand aside."

Don't let your body go out of control and think that it will not have eternal consequences. Run the best spiritual race you can, so that you glorify God and shame the devil.

12. Cast off all sin. You do not have to live like others any more. God has freed you from that.

Colossians 2:11 (TLB): "When you came to Christ he set you free from your evil desires, not only by a bodily operation of circumcision but by a spiritual operation, the baptism of your souls."

Once and for all God has freed you. Today you can start to live as if that were true—because it is. Hate evil and love what is good. Show it by the way you treat your body!

9

Am I What I Do?

Can you imagine going to school with Jesus? After all, when he was twelve years old, he pointed out to the temple priests some things they hadn't noticed about God. Even though he didn't have "body beautiful," he could do a lot. He had many talents.

You don't have to be able to tell the leaders of your church all about God in order to be important to him. He's created you with your own set of talents and your own personality. Though you might not win a prize at the county fair, come in first place at a talent contest, win a full scholarship to the college of your choice, or be voted class favorite, you have something to offer the world, too. It can be hard work to find and use those talents, but it will also make you feel good about yourself, if you keep your attitudes in balance.

Talents

You don't need to win a talent show to know that you're better at some things than others or to know that you can do some things your friends or family don't want to bother with. Each of us has some special abilities that make us unique in our homes, schools, and communities. Knowing that we can do some things well shows us that we are special, and we can feel good about ourselves because of that.

To begin to discover your own talents, take this simple test.

Talent Scout

1. *Write down all the things you really like to do.* Name things that make you feel good when you spend time at them. Here's a list that will help you get started:

Building things	Singing
Organizing trips	Playing games
Playing ball	Reading
Giving parties	Talking
Windsurfing	Fishing
Listening to others	Skiing
Sailing	Doing puzzles
Playing an instrument	Skating
Acting	Working with tools
Public speaking	Caring for children
Running	Teaching others
Gardening	Writing
Sewing	Computing

2. *What comes easily to you?* Normally our talents show up in places where we have an easy time. If you like to write, you won't mind spending time at your computer, setting out stories. A friend of mine has a son who is a natural golfer. Because he enjoys it, he practices a lot.

3. *What do you spend time doing?* What activities have you been drawn to since you were a child? Perhaps you like to swim, and summertime always finds you in the

water. No one has to talk you into doing it, because it just seems fun.

4. *What do people praise you for?* If you like something, you are going to do well in it. The more people notice and praise you, the more encouraged you will feel to try it.

5. *What do you dream of doing when you grow up?* Would you like to be a doctor, work with kids, be in sports, or go to another country as a missionary? If you have felt that way for a number of years, God may be drawing out your natural talent. Because you have great skill in it, it's a logical goal.

6. *What can you practice for a long period of time?* If you hate playing the piano, chances are you'll never make it as a concert pianist. You'd suffer through practice; you'd just have to force yourself too much. If you love it, though, you can keep at it for long enough to build your skill.

7. *Does it benefit others?* Of course you can practice lying and stealing, but that doesn't mean they should be part of your future career. Before you accept your goal, ask if it is good for you, others, and society. Does God approve of it?

Perhaps you discovered some talents you'd never suspected you had. Did you find some areas I hadn't listed that make your life happier, more fun, and interesting? I hope so.

As you try new things, you may discover career areas you never would have expected. Or maybe you'll just add a hobby to your life.

Art had always liked math in school, but he had no idea what he wanted to do for a career. His senior year he took courses in economics and statistics and knew he'd found his future. While other teens had trouble working out the figures and understanding what they meant, he enjoyed it. "I never would have guessed that I'd like economics," he told his guidance counselor. "But I sure am glad you suggested that I take the course. Now I know where I want to go to college."

Angela had almost slept through a whole year of biology. *What use do I have for this?* she wondered the whole time. But one summer, when her grandfather got ill, she offered to help her grandmother with the vegetable garden Gramps had started before he went into the hospital. "I never understood all that stuff about photosynthesis, and I don't think I could ever get a degree in science," she told her grandmother. "But I liked getting out here and watering the plants, digging the weeds, and watching the tomatoes get ripe. It was a lot of work, but next year I want Gramps to teach me how to plant my own garden, because I had so much fun." She may never own a farm or discover new kinds of plants, but Angela's got a hobby that she can share with people who need food. She learned to can the tomatoes her family couldn't eat and gave them to her church pantry, to help homeless families in her area.

Whatever your natural talents, discover and make use of them. You've got your own special combination of likes and dislikes, thoughts, and abilities. God has made them for you to share. Once you have a direction, make the most of it.

Am I Just a Bunch of Talents?

It's fun to discover what you're good at. Knowing you can excel at things will give you a boost of enthusiasm. Don't become so involved in achieving, however, that you place pressure on yourself to be perfect or begin to think you are only valuable because of what you do. You own your talents—don't let them own you. You are important because of whose you are—God's—not who you are.

Getting good grades, making it into the school play, and winning the election for class president may all be good goals. Still, if you don't achieve them, God hasn't given up on you. When all that's important is what you do, you've forgotten that God loves you just as you are. Even if you couldn't pick up a pencil, sing well enough to be in a musical, or get the vote out, he'd love you. He chose to love you a long time ago, and he doesn't change his mind. He has a goal for your life that you may not even be able to see right now.

So enjoy the things you do well—let them build up the knowledge that God loves you enough to give you the gift of talents. Remember, though, God gave you love before he gave you talents. They are only part of you, and they could never earn his love. Gifts are for sharing, so share yours with the world. Then thank God that he gave them to you.

10

What's in My Name?

You can bet that the people around Galilee knew Jesus and what he stood for. Even though no one picked him out as the Son of God before he was baptized by John, they must have known that he didn't do some things. After all, who could imagine God's Son cheating on a test, lying to his neighbor, or spreading gossip about a friend? Someone in Galilee would have been quick to point out such failings, once he'd heard about this new Messiah.

Having a good reputation was important to where Jesus wanted to go in life, so he built his stature on good attitudes and deeds. Though you won't be perfect, you, too, need a good reputation that will help you through the years.

How Do I Build a Good Reputation?

Much of your reputation will come from the things you do. When you are active in your church group, school clubs, or community efforts, you'll get known to people. If they see that you achieve well and that you make wise decisions, they'll think well of you.

If you do things that don't earn respect, you'll earn a reputation for doing the wrong thing, for choosing unwisely, and people will not think highly of you. Today lots of people may scoff at the idea that you need a good reputation.

When Rick encouraged Sally to have sex with him and she turned him down, he asked, "You don't care what other people think, do you?"

Sally thought a moment. She didn't want him to get the idea that she was influenced easily by others, but the fact was that she did care about her reputation. "Yes," she answered. "I guess I do care what others think. I'm a Christian, and I don't want to do anything that would make Jesus look bad. When people know what I believe and see me doing something wrong, they won't appreciate him."

That situation made Sally think about why she dated Rick. If he thought having sex was okay, they didn't share an understanding of what was right and wrong. In a little while, she decided she didn't want to date Rick if it meant risking having sex with him.

Sally made a wise decision. The Bible advises: "If you must choose, take a good name rather than great riches; for to be held in loving esteem is better than silver and gold" (Prov. 22:1 TLB). Though she hadn't read that verse recently, she knew its principle and held to it when life pressured her. Though she missed Rick for a while, in the end she knew she could not have lived with herself if she had given in to his demands. As she spent time with the other teens in her church youth group, she felt encouraged that, though she had given up a few dates, she had made others respect her. "I don't have to date to like myself. If it's a choice between feeling good about myself and going out on a Friday night, I'll do the thing that builds my self-esteem," she shared with a friend.

For Fred, it wasn't a matter of dating, but of doing well in school. Though his teachers said he could get high grades, he never seemed to. There was always a game to go to, a friend who needed help, or a job to do at home. Homework always seemed at the bottom of his list.

Finally a counselor pointed out to Fred that his chances for getting into college were slipping away. "Sure you can go out and work, once you finish high school. But is that the kind of future you want for yourself? Getting a job at McDonald's seems fine now, but you can't support a family on what you'd make there, and you won't have many skills to offer an employer. You'll make more money once you have an education, and you have the brains to do it. I hate to see you waste your chances because you don't want to do homework."

Fred thought about that and started making some changes. He still kept in touch with his friends, but only after he'd finished his homework. Now instead of spending one hour studying for a test, he spends a whole night. The difference in his grades is startling, and so is the change in the opinion of his teachers.

"I knew you could do it," said his counselor. "You've got a lot to share with other people, as long as you do it the best way. I'd be happy to see you counseling people for a living—you seem to do it naturally—but don't let that get in the way of the goals you need to set today."

Changing Your Reputation

Do you need to develop a new reputation? Start today, using a simple four-step plan.

1. Discover what you've done wrong. Fred and Sally had been making some unwise choices that they needed to change. Before they could change, however, they had to identify the problem. Don't be like Fred and wait for someone to walk up to you and tell you. Take a look at your own life and head off the problems.

Have people told you they think you're making a mistake? Have they tried to steer you away from a decision? Think through their advice and evaluate where you are today. Were they right? Do you find yourself in a place you hate, because you made a bad choice? Go back, look at your mistake, and see what you need to do to correct it.

2. Make amends, if necessary. Lyle had lied to his father about the places he went on Saturdays. Now they didn't talk about where he went on the weekends, but Lyle's relationship with his father was hurting.

After he accepted Jesus, Lyle knew he had to apologize to his dad.

"Dad," he said, "I know I've been wrong in the places I've gone and the things I've done on the weekend. I'm sorry for that—and I'm even more sorry that I lied to you about it. Can you forgive me?"

Lyle's father forgave him, but it took a while to reestablish trust between them. Every weekend Lyle made sure his dad knew what was going on. He even spent some time at home. When his dad saw that Lyle was where he said he'd be, he knew his son had changed. Now they have a better life together.

Do you need to apologize, give back something you've stolen, or make up to someone for a mistake? Only by admitting you were wrong and taking responsibility for your mistake can you bring healing to a broken relationship. You may have to give the other person time, just as Lyle didn't see the full measure of his dad's forgiveness for a while, but with patience and faithfulness, you may have a better relationship. If things don't work out, at least you will have the peace that you have done your best. Leave guilt behind and move on in faith.

3. Develop a new plan. Once you know what you've done wrong and have identified your mistakes, make a plan that will keep you from repeating the mistakes. For Sally that meant deciding not to date someone who did not share her faith in Christ. "I thought Rick had some faith, but I was wrong. What happened between us convinced me I need to choose dates more carefully. Now I get to know someone a little before I go out with him. If he does not share my values and beliefs, I feel free to turn him down." She may not date as much as before, but Sally is happier in her new plan. "When a boy treats you well, you have a much better dating relationship. Now that I'm seeing David, I know what was wrong between Rick and me."

4. Put your plan into action. When Lyle decided to be honest with his parents, he made it a practice to call them when he changed his plans. It was a pain at times to have to stop and call, but that made his parents trust him. If they needed to call him, they knew where he was. On the occasions when they did call, he proved he was trustworthy. Eventually the cost of a few phone calls paid a great bonus. The new relationship with his parents is something Lyle never thought could happen. "I couldn't give enough money to have this kind of family life," Lyle shared. "A short time of trouble is worth it."

Improving Your Reputation

Perhaps you don't have a problem with stealing, lying, or cheating. You don't need to have a "big" problem to get a reputation you'd like to change.

"I'd gotten a reputation for being a real snob," Beth shared. "People thought I didn't think much of them, but the real person I doubted was myself. *Will people like me?* I kept wondering, and I wanted them to. I just felt afraid to open up to them.

"Finally I took a look at what my life's really like. When I make friends, I keep them for a long time. People like me when they get to know me, but I make it hard for them to do that.

"Saying hello or adding to someone's conversation takes courage for me, but I try to do it anyway. Now I know I do have something to offer and that people want to know me, and I'm reaching out in spite of my doubts. You know, there are a lot of nice people out there—and I used to turn them off!"

Is your own attitude getting in your way? Take a look at the way you think about yourself and others—and how you treat people. Which of these describe you?

People Quiz

___ 1. I like people and treat them as if they are important.

___ 2. I am afraid of others and what they might do to me or say about me.

___ 3. When others share their feelings, I listen carefully and give them good feedback.

___ 4. When a friend has a problem and comes to me, he wants answers. I jump right in with all the advice I can give.

___ 5. If someone compliments me for a good job, I say, "Thank you," politely.

___ 6. When someone says I've done well, I respond, "Oh, anyone could do that."

___ 7. If a friend is quiet, I try to invite her into my conversation.

___ 8. I always have good ideas, so when I talk I tell others about them. If anyone else wants to say something, it's too bad.

___ 9. I learn from other people, so I like to listen to their ideas.

__ 10. Other people always have better ideas than mine. If my ideas are any good, someone else will eventually come up with them.

__ 11. People who are different from me are interesting. I like to discover what they are like.

__ 12. People who aren't my friends aren't my type. If I don't spend time with them, it won't matter.

__ 13. My family is important to me. Even if it isn't perfect, I want it to be as good as possible. I'll spend time to make it that way.

__ 14. My family doesn't matter at all, but my friends do. I won't be at home, if I can go out with my buddies.

Make an effort to develop the attitudes in the odd-numbered answers on the above quiz. Do you:

- Listen carefully to others
- Encourage people when they feel down
- Share your own problems with friends
- Try not to complain about every little trouble
- Accept people who don't agree with you, look like you, or have your background
- Do what you can to develop a strong family life
- Appreciate people when they are kind to you or try to help you
- Understand that no one is perfect

If you focus on others, treat them with respect, and encourage them, you will build their respect. If you complain and tear them down, you will build a reputation for being difficult.

How do people see you? As easy to talk to, kind, gentle, and considerate, or complaining, angry, and belligerent? Which would you rather be? Now is the time to take stock of yourself and develop the communication skills that can help you for a lifetime. Maybe you need to learn to listen more caringly, share your own problems with someone who can help, or improve your own opinion of yourself.

Remember, you can grow in stature. Twenty years from now, no one wants the same stature he has today. If it seems as if you have a lot of work to do, start now. You don't need to stay the same, and a better name is just waiting for you.

11

God Who?

"God didn't mean much to me until I met Susan," Barbie explained. "At home I'd always heard that he was love, but I just missed out on the message. I'm sure my parents tried, but I couldn't see it the way I did with Susan."

It's hard for us to understand God, and chances are that you see him as being much like the major authority figures in your life. The reason for that is that we humans learn more easily by example than we do by words. If your dad says God is loving, caring, and concerned but spends all his time at the church, leaving your family to fend for itself, you will see God as someone who can't spend much time with you either. Maybe he will seem as if he just doesn't care or can't be bothered.

The good news is that even if your mom and dad don't show you his love, God can reach you. He isn't the mean man in the sky, waiting to pounce on your sins, the "clockmaker God" who made the world and then gave up on it, or a careless father who has forgotten about his children.

Who Is God Really?

Is God a meanie who wants to pick on our mistakes, or does he simply pat us on the back and tell us to do better whenever we sin? Though many people do see him in either of those ways, they have missed out on two key points in God's nature:

1. God is *just.* When we do wrong, we are accountable for it. We cannot avoid that, and he doesn't sweep our mistakes under the rug. But if he were only just, we'd all be in big trouble.
2. God is also *gracious.* That means he knows that we can't pay the price for our own mistakes (or sins), so he has given us another way. "For it is by grace you have been saved, through faith . . ." the Bible promises (Eph. 2:8). When Jesus died on the cross, he died for all our sins, even the ones we have yet to commit.

Knowing God doesn't mean you can sit back and live any way you please and get away with it. You haven't bought a convenient fire-insurance package that keeps you from hell as long as you pay a cheap premium. Knowing God is costly. Once he is in your heart, you will not feel comfortable with sin. Your tender conscience will hurt when you do not follow him.

Know God better, and you will understand what he is like. To deepen your life with him, follow these three steps:

1. Become aware of who God is. Take time to get to know God by reading his Word, the Bible. He has given us a rule book that steers us away from mistakes that cause suffering and pain. Get to know what God wants in your life—and out of it—by studying his Word, learning what he says, and putting it into your life.

2. Desire God. Once you know who he is, you must seek to serve him with your whole life. Instead of trying to hide from him, tell Jesus that you want to be his person—to follow him every day, in all you do.

When you follow him, be prepared to stand out in a crowd, because you'll do things differently from most other people. Instead of serving yourself, you'll be concerned about God and his will. You won't follow the crowd, and at times the narrow path of obedience to God may seem to bring you few other friends, but going along with the crowd takes little effort—and gives you few rewards.

3. Take action. Once you know who God is and have a desire to serve him, you need to act out the truth. Your head may tell you that God is cold and uncaring, like your father, but you need to reject that untruth by believing what his Word says and acting it out in your life. Instead of trying to ignore God before he can ignore you, spend time with him, telling him of your feelings. Learn how you become a more caring, less bitter person, and you will begin to feel his new life within you.

Twelve Reasons to Trust God

You can really trust God. Why? Have you ever thought just what he is like? Just as you know a friend well and can tell what he will do because you appreciate his character, you can be sure of God, because you know him well.

1. God is omnipotent. He has all power and can do all things—except lie. ". . . It is impossible for God to lie . . ." (Heb. 6:18). So when he makes a promise to you, he means it. You can trust that it will happen.

If you've had your dad lie to you, or if a teacher has hurt you by avoiding the truth, you may feel as if God lies, too. Remember, though, that those adults are not

God. When you blame their mistakes on him, you have been fooled by a lie.

No matter what the situation, God has not lost control. He is still powerful. ". . . Praise the Lord. For the Lord our God, the Almighty, reigns" (Rev. 19:6 TLB). When a friend dies, your family fails you, or life seems unfair, remember that you cannot see the whole picture. One day, when you can, you may understand. Until then, place your hope in God—he never lies!

2. He is omnipresent. Because God is not governed by bodily contact, but by a relationship, he is everywhere at one time.

> *Psalm 139:7–12 (TLB):* "I can never be lost to your Spirit! I can never get away from my God! If I go up to heaven, you are there; if I go down to the place of the dead, you are there. If I ride the morning winds to the farthest oceans, even there your hand will guide me, your strength will support me. If I try to hide in the darkness, the night becomes light around me. For even darkness cannot hide from God; to you the night shines as bright as day. Darkness and light are both alike to you."

No matter where you go, you can't avoid God. He is in heaven and hell—even darkness can't keep you from him. Running away won't work.

3. God is omniscient. He knows everything about us, our world, and our universe.

> *Psalm 139:13–16 (TLB):* "You made all the delicate, inner parts of my body, and knit them together in my mother's womb. Thank you for making me so wonderfully complex! It is amazing to think about. Your workmanship is marvelous—and how well I know it. You were there while I was being formed in utter seclusion! You saw me before I was born and scheduled each day of

my life before I began to breathe. Every day was recorded in your Book!"

Before you were born, God knew you. With what attention to detail he made each part of you! his works are wonderful—and you are one of them. You weren't somehow made while he was away, busy somewhere. He knows every piece of you—how you are made, how you think, and what bothers you. Since he already has the key to your makeup, you can trust in him. Tell him all, since he knows it anyway. He's just waiting for you to share it with him.

4. God is perfect. Anything that is not perfect comes from sin and rebellion, because God is perfect.

> *Deuteronomy 32:4 (TLB):* "He is the Rock. His work is perfect. Everything he does is just and fair. He is faithful, without sin."

> *Psalm 18:30 (TLB):* "What a God he is! How perfect in every way! All his promises prove true. He is a shield for everyone who hides behind him."

When we make decisions, we may choose not to go in God's perfect way. That cannot change his nature, and we can't blame him when we mess up.

> *Matthew 5:48 (TLB):* "But you are to be perfect, even as your Father in heaven is perfect."

On earth we will never make it to perfection. Do you know a teacher, parent, or relative who has never made a mistake, said a harsh word, or done something he regretted? No. We all fail in one way or another, every day. In heaven we will be perfect, like God. Today it takes faith to believe in a perfect God when those around you—and you yourself—fail so often. God isn't like your best friend, parents, or teacher. He's much bigger and better than they could ever be.

5. *God is life.* We may think we are living, because our hearts beat, we breathe in and out, and it takes food to keep us going. Compared to God, we don't even begin to know what life is as long as we only do the physical things of life.

> *John 5:26, 27 (TLB):* "The Father has life in himself, and has granted his Son to have life in himself, and to judge the sins of all mankind because he is the Son of Man."

God gives us new life—eternal life—when we accept Jesus as our Lord. He is life, and he knows how to give it to us.

6. *God is truth.* Without him, you can be misled into all kinds of mistaken ideas and actions. But he is the one and only God, who is true. You don't have to ponder whether or not he exists, whether there is a better God, or whether he has the best offer for the afterlife.

> John 17:3 *(TLB):* "And this is the way to have eternal life— by knowing you, the only true God, and Jesus Christ, the one you sent to earth!"

> 1 John 5:20, 21 *(TLB):* "And we know that Christ, God's Son, has come to help us understand and find the true God. And now we are in God because we are in Jesus Christ his Son, who is the only true God; and he is eternal life.
>
> "Dear children, keep away from anything that might take God's place in your hearts. Amen."

What might take God's place in your heart? An idol— anything that you'll try to love more than him. Do not let others mislead you. Instead, guard yourself by reading God's Word and spending time with him. As you hide his Word in your heart and get to know him better, you will grow in faith and avoid idols.

7. God is wise. Nothing gets past God because he can't understand it or doesn't know where to go from here. He makes the best decisions in the world.

> *Romans 11:33 (TLB):* "Oh, what a wonderful God we have! How great are His wisdom and knowledge and riches! How impossible it is for us to understand his decisions and his methods!"

> *1 Timothy 1:17 (TLB):* "Glory and honor to God forever and ever. He is the King of the ages, the unseen one who never dies; he alone is God, and full of wisdom. Amen."

We have only got a small store of knowledge, based on our experiences. Though we try to take the right actions, make good decisions, and help others well, we run into situations we can't control. That's when we need to borrow God's wisdom.

When we feel as if we have no more solutions left in our family lives, friendships, and futures, we can turn to him for the answers.

8. God is love. Because he loves us so deeply, God communicates his infinite goodness to us.

> *John 3:16 (TLB):* "For God loved the world so much that he gave his only Son so that anyone who believes in him shall not perish but have eternal life."

> *Romans 15:30 (TLB):* "Will you be my prayer partners? For the Lord Jesus Christ's sake, and because of your love for me—given to you by the Holy Spirit—pray much with me for my work."

> *1 John 4:8 (TLB):* "But if a person isn't loving and kind, it shows that he doesn't know God—for God is love."

Knowing God means sharing his love with others. Not only will he give us his love, he expects us to draw others into our loving circle. There's no such thing as a Lone Ranger Christian, who won't go out of his way for anyone else. Sooner or later, God's love will show through— or others will know that person never believed at all.

9. God is holy. You can trust God because his entire nature is pure. No spots or blemishes keep him from doing the right thing at all times. He'll never let you down by doing something self-serving or convenient.

> *Exodus 15:11 (TLB):* "Who else is like the Lord among the gods? Who is glorious in holiness like him? Who is so awesome in splendor, a wonder-working God?"
>
> *Isaiah 6:3 (TLB):* "In a great antiphonal chorus they sang, 'Holy, holy, holy is the Lord of Hosts; the whole earth is filled with his glory.'"
>
> *1 Peter 1:16 (TLB):* "He himself has said, 'You must be holy, for I am holy.'"

When we follow in his footsteps, we show that he makes us pure, too. We don't have to do things that hurt others, simply because we want our own way.

10. God is faithful. He will never let you down, even if you let him down. God won't change at all, because he must always be true to you.

> *1 Corinthians 10:13:* "No temptation has seized you except what is common to man. And God is faithful; he will not let you be tempted beyond what you can bear. But when you are tempted, he will also provide a way out so that you can stand up under it."
>
> *2 Corinthians 1:20 (TLB):* "He carries out and fulfills all of God's promises, no matter how many of them there are; and we have told everyone how faithful he is, giving glory to his name."

Hebrews 6:18 (TLB): "He has given us both his promise and his oath, two things we can completely count on, for it is impossible for God to tell a lie. Now all those who flee to him to save them can take new courage when they hear such assurances from God; now they can know without doubt that he will give them the salvation he has promised them."

11. God is merciful. We don't have to suffer unnecessarily, because he gives us his mercy.

2 Corinthians 1:2: "Grace and peace to you from God our Father and the Lord Jesus Christ."

Titus 3:5, 6: "He saved us, not because of righteous things we had done, but because of his mercy. He saved us through the washing of rebirth and renewal by the Holy Spirit, whom he poured out on us generously through Jesus Christ our Savior."

When we most needed his forgiveness, God gave it to us, through Jesus. Instead of punishing us, he sent his Son to die for us, only out of mercy.

12. God is good. God's goodness outclasses ours any day.

Psalm 86:5: "You are forgiving and good, O Lord, abounding in love to all who call to you."

Psalm 119:68: "You are good, and what you do is good. . . ."

How can any of us claim to only do good? We fail all the time, yet God has stayed faithful to us.

With twelve good reasons like that to trust God, why would you want to doubt him? Do you have a friend anywhere who can treat you as well as God does?

Get to know God well and you will love him more deeply. As you see what he has done for you, you will feel humbled and thankful. You will know that nothing on earth can compare to him.

Next we'll take a look at how you can draw closer to God by avoiding some mistakes and bringing a few good things into your life.

12

If God's So Big, Why Am I So Bad?

What if you were the strongest man in the world—and you knew you only had your strength because God had given it to you? Would you be careful about staying close to him? Would you want to follow pagan people, or would you put God first in your life?

Before you answer quickly, think about it. It might be harder than you think to be different, even if you were strong. In this story, God has given us an example of how our own power wears out if we don't put him first in our lives. You can find the true-life story of this strong man in Judges 14–16—it tells about Samson.

We aren't talking about some wimpy guy dressed up in a sheet here. Samson killed a lion with his bare hands. Once, when his enemies got him angry, he killed a thousand men with a donkey jaw! Even without a semi-automatic in his hands, this guy was deadly.

But even Israel's strong man was not invincible when he made bad choices. His parents told him to marry a girl who loved God, but Samson ignored their advice. A nice-looking girl from the Philistines had caught his eye, and he was determined to have her. Before long, the strong man was more interested in doing what his unbelieving wife wanted than serving God.

Read Judges 14–16 to see the kind of influence a few bad choices had on Samson's life. As you go through the story, circle any ideas that apply to you.

Avoiding Spiritual Pitfalls

When you need to make decisions, it's as if you had come to a fork in the road. Unfortunately, you won't find a sign saying, "This way is good. You'll have a wonderful future if you follow this path." The other way doesn't have a sign advertising, "This looks exciting, but you will hurt terribly if you go this way. You will be afraid and have pain, and the memories of your travels here will always make you sad." If you did see such signs, you'd know for sure which way to travel in your own best interests. When you did take the bad road, just for kicks, at least you would be warned.

Samson didn't have any signs, either. Nevertheless, he had been warned by God and other believers. Ignoring those warnings cost him a lot. His wife tricked him, and in the end he was blind and had to be led by a small child. The strong man had become very weak physically and spiritually. Had Samson made better choices, he might not have had all that suffering.

Everyone has the chance to make his own decisions. Even when life's out of control, following God is still the best answer to any problem.

What if you were your father's favorite child? While Dad bragged about you all the time, your brothers got madder and madder. Finally they had had it and took their chance to sell you into slavery. You suffered, even though you hadn't made any bad choices. Still, God stayed with you, and you became the right-hand man of a powerful noble. Then just when things were going well, the noble's wife wanted to have sex with you. When you refused her, because God says it's wrong, she lied about you, saying you'd done just what you refused. So you went to prison.

That's what happened to Joseph, whose story is in Genesis 37–50. The story doesn't end there, though. While he sat in prison, Joseph kept on being faithful to God. Soon he was in charge of other prisoners. Then God gave him a chance to help two men who had dreams. He told them what their dreams meant, and one day he had a chance to interpret a dream for the ruler of Egypt. Suddenly Joseph was his right-hand man!

When famine came, Joseph's brothers traveled to Egypt to get food—and it was up to Joseph whether or not they got it. Then even when he had the chance to pay back the people who had made him suffer for so long, Joseph forgave them.

What a valuable lesson for a messed-up family life! Forgiveness in the face of great pain must have been hard for Joseph, but he was committed to God.

Bible Study

Here are some other stories that can help you make wise choices. Read and study them.

1. Read the story of David and Goliath (you'll find it in 1 Samuel 17). Then ask yourself:
   - What had God already saved David from? How did that help him fight Goliath?

   - Why did David have confidence that he could win over this mighty giant?

- What has God already saved me from? Do I have something in my past, present, or future that I need help with?

- Why can I have confidence that God will help me win over the giants in my life?

- Do I need to do something (to stop sinning in some way, to ask for forgiveness, or to do something I've been putting off) before God can really work in my life?

- Do I need to go out and confront some giants in my own life? How can I be better prepared for the situation?

2. Read the Christmas story in Matthew 2. Ask yourself:
   - What kind of effort did the wise men make to seek Jesus? Was it easy for them to find him? What did they give up to visit him?

   - When the wise men met Jesus, what did they give to him? Were their gifts expensive or cheap? Did they give him the best or something secondhand?

   - What effort do I make to know Jesus? Do I seek him only when it's convenient, or do I travel with him all the way?

   - What kind of gifts do I give to Jesus? Do I do it every day, or every three or four years? Do I only look for him when I'm hanging on the edge of a cliff, or do I serve him when life is going well?

- What gifts do I need to give Jesus today?

3. Read Matthew 6 and ask:
   - Am I worrying about things that I cannot control in my life? About things I can control? List each one.

   - What attitude should I have about the things I cannot control? How do I know that God will care for them? What does he want for me?

   - What do I need to do about the things I worry about that I can control? Are there parts of them I cannot control? How can I react to that situation?

4. Read Exodus 14 and ask:
   - How did Moses feel when he was trapped by the Red Sea, and the Egyptians came rolling along in their war chariots?

   - What response did the people have when they saw the Egyptians coming?

   - What did God say to Moses, when he heard their crying?

   - Have I ever felt as if I was stranded by God, with no one caring and the world crushing me? Did God leave me stranded in that situation?

- Do I need to take action to change my situation, just as Moses did? What is the solution I need to take part in?

From these stories, I hope you can see that even when life seems impossible—when you've made the biggest mistake ever or when others have made it for you—there is hope.

Maybe you've asked yourself, *If God's so big, why am I so bad?* Seems as if a huge, wonderful God like that should just zap you into perfection, doesn't it? Sure, we'd all like instant perfection—we're used to fast food, fast money, and fast cars. But God works slowly and surely to make us like him. Like trees, he wants us to grow all summer, store up our sap during the winter, and grow again when the spring comes. That way we can get tall and strong, with our roots deep in him. He's growing something mighty, not just a flower that will die when the frost hits.

Tapping into God

To become the kind of healthy tree God wants in his forest, start getting serious about where you want to go spiritually. In the next few pages, we'll look at some strategies for spiritual growth that can help every teen.

1. Read God's love letter daily. To help you know him better, God has given you his Word, the Bible. He gives you the straight facts, his ideas, and his ideals in its pages. To grow in him, you need to be tapped into his Word.

Don't read the Bible only because you feel that he will get angry with you if you don't. Read it to understand him, to learn how to live to glorify him, to avoid trouble in your own life, and to feel close to him. Make the Bible your rule book for action.

You can be a student of the Bible if you try to learn all you can from it. Don't dip into it once a week, "just to make God happy." Squeeze all the great truths from it, just the way you'd try to get all the juice from a delicious orange. Dig into the Word, so you'll understand the basics and then move on to more complicated truths.

How can you tell if you are a student? Students really study. They have a serious goal, and they will do a lot to get knowledge. If you are a Bible student, no one should have to tell you to read your Bible: You will want to do it.

Is it too much trouble to pick up the Word? Then you aren't really God's student. Take time to get with him and discuss your problem. He can give you the desire you need.

2. Hide God's Word in your heart. If you read it and forget it, you won't really know God's Word. So when you find a verse that means a lot to you, jot it down and memorize it—hide it in your heart. Repeat it out loud. If you memorize Scripture, it will stay with you when you need it. You'll have something to hold on to when you are tempted to doubt, when you face a need, or when someone attacks you.

Remember when Jesus was in the desert, being tempted by Satan? The devil wanted him to turn stones into bread. Jesus was hungry—and the food probably sounded like a good idea. But he came back with Scripture, "Man does not live on bread alone, but on every word that comes from the mouth of God" (Matt. 4:4). Just as the Lord was prepared with a memorized verse from the Old Testament, you can answer the temptations of Satan by knowing his Word.

3. Read devotions on a regular basis. God's Word isn't stuffed in mothballs, because it's so old. He has given us what we need for today in the Bible. Read devotions that will point you toward God and help you know him better.

When I wrote *Outtakes for Guys, Outtakes for Girls, Goalposts for Guys,* and *Goalposts for Girls,* I tried to keep them to a five- to fifteen-minute reading that would show teens how God lives today and cares for them. These and other good books can fire you up for God.

4. Find life verses. When you feel as if life is tough, look for a verse that describes what you are going through. A concordance can help you discover verses that talk about your problem.

When I get criticized for mentioning God in my school programs, I hold on to Romans 8:18 (TLB): "Yet what we suffer now is nothing compared to the glory he will give us later." That verse helps me keep my eyes on the future God has for me and the glory I will see when I am in his presence.

I can also speak out boldly when I focus on these verses:

> *Acts 18:9, 10 (TLB):* "One night the Lord spoke to Paul in a vision and told him, 'Don't be afraid!' Speak out! Don't quit! For I am with you and no one can harm you. Many people here in this city belong to me.'"

> *Romans 1:16 (TLB):* "For I am not ashamed of this Good News about Christ. It is God's powerful method of bringing all who believe it to heaven. This message was preached first to the Jews alone, but now everyone is invited to come to God in this same way."

Find verses that mean a lot to you and memorize them. Use them again and again as you face similar situations.

5. With what Bible character do you identify? Are you like Peter, who spoke out boldly—but often put his foot in his mouth? Maybe you are like Matthew, who came when God called, leaving his business behind. Are you like Thomas, who had to see before he would believe? Or maybe you are like beautiful, innocent, faith-filled Mary, who became the mother of God's Son. Find someone in the Bible to whom you can relate. What can you learn from that person's life?

6. *Become part of a loving, caring, Bible-believing church.* If you become really involved in church, you can make a difference. Some teens in my church are vitally important to the body. They have real fellowship, and others benefit from that. Don't stand alone in the faith, or you won't stand for long. Fellowship will help you grow and keep you close to God.

7. *Get involved with a vital youth group that lives for the Lord.* Find one that has fun while it learns about living for God and sharing the Good News of Jesus Christ. Do not get involved with a group that encourages gossips or cliques, but choose one that works for the Lord. If your church does not have a group, talk to other youth pastors in your area. Discover Christians your age and a youth leader who really wants to help teens.

8. *Attend a Christian camp.* Many teens have told me that a camp experience helped solidify their faith. Others may come to faith in Christ, rededicate their lives to him, or deepen their knowledge of God while they spend time at a good Christian camp.

Away from your everyday pressures, you may really focus on who the Lord is and what he means to you. Come to grips with the fact that you only go around once in life and that living for God is the greatest challenge. The most daring thing a teen can do is live for Christ.

Following Jesus means a lot more than wearing a cross around your neck. Your whole life has to show what you believe. Get serious with God by spending some time with him at camp. If you are close to him, become a counselor. Seeing others get excited about him will help you through the rest of your life.

9. Teach Sunday school. Take on a class of younger students for a short time—maybe three months. You will learn dedication and commitment—and about God. Studying your lesson beforehand, giving it, and thinking about it on your way home from church will reinforce the ideas three times. Teachers always grow more than their students.

You'll feel needed as you encourage students to memorize their verses, learn about God, and grow in him. They need your example to watch, so they can see what Jesus is like.

10. Listen to good Christian music. Each time I listen to Christian music, I grow in my faith, so I've bought a big collection of tapes and CDs. Different styles minister to me. There are many good Christian musicians out there today, with a quality that equals any secular work (and Christian lyrics have always been better than the secular ones). If you don't like the music you have heard, find some you do enjoy.

11. Keep a journal. Every day, in a book you buy just for this, write a short letter to God, thanking him for all he has done for you, confessing your sins, and asking his help.

Journal Entry

Dear God:

Good morning! Today I spent a few moments reading Your Bible. Thank You for the message You have given me in Psalm 92:1, 2 (TLB): "It is good to say thank you to the Lord, to sing praises to the God who is above all gods. Every morning tell him thank you for your kindness, and every evening rejoice in all his faithfulness."

Lord, I want to thank You for walking with me through each day. Yesterday was pretty tough, when I had to stand up for my faith in school, but You gave me the words to say. Even though they didn't seem to have much impact, I thank You that I could stand up for You, to make others think about You.

You give me so many blessings and opportunities that I cannot count them. So often I forget to say thank You, but You still give them to me.

Yesterday I noticed how proud I was when I was with my friends. Jesus, I don't want to do that again. When John tried to tell me how he felt, I just went on with my own words. Later I realized how much I'd hurt his feelings. Forgive me, God, and help me to be sensitive to the needs of others.

Thank You for listening to me, guiding me, and guarding me today. Thank You for loving me and being my Creator, Lord, Savior, and Best Friend. I'll talk with You tomorrow!

Don't make journal-entry time a period of guilt and pain. When you review your failings, ask forgiveness and believe that God has given it. Thank him for all he has done for you, too. Make this a blessed time between you and God.

12. Pray all the time. By that I don't mean give up your schoolwork, your job, and your family time in order to sit in a corner and pray. You can often talk to God in the middle of a test, while you walk home from a friend's house, or when you face a tough decision. Don't stop your life for faith, but keep exercising it in the middle of life.

Set aside regular times for serious prayer, too. Each day remember to thank God for what he has done for you, confess your sins, and share your troubles with him. He's waiting for you to talk to him in the middle of a busy day.

God's *Be's* for Believers

What is the goal of doing Bible study, spending time with other Christians, and praying? It's not so you can set up rules, check up on each other, and see how tough your knees are! God wants you to know him and become a certain kind of person.

The New Testament has seventy-four *be's,* that describe the Christian. I'd like to share three with you. Follow these, and you will feel great about yourself and what God has done for you.

1. Be glad when you are persecuted for your faith. That's a tough one. No one likes to be criticized for what he or she believes. Yet God says there is a blessing even in that.

> *Matthew 5:11, 12:* "Blessed are you when people insult you . . . because of me. Rejoice and be glad, because great is your reward in heaven, for in the same way they persecuted the prophets who were before you."

When someone calls you "Preacher," makes fun of your morality, or says there is no God, just to make you mad, be glad. You'll be counted as one of the great heroes of the faith, because they, too, were scoffed at.

2. Be reconciled to other people. If you need to ask forgiveness and make things right between you and a friend, family member, or acquaintance, do it.

> *Matthew 5:23, 24:* "Therefore, if you are offering your gift at the altar and there remember that your brother has something against you, leave your gift there in front of the altar. First go and be reconciled to your brother; then come and offer your gift."

Before you can "play church," you need to take care of any wrongdoing. How much worry would leave your life if you could just ask for forgiveness from someone else? Whom have you:

- Gossiped about
- Made fun of
- Argued with
- Lashed out at in anger
- Fought with
- Cut down

You'll feel better if you make peace with these people. Your mind and heart will not hold on to worries, and you will feel comfortable again with the Lord. You'll like yourself better, as a result.

3. Be wise as a snake and harmless as a dove. Jesus knew what the world is like out there.

Matthew 10:16: "I am sending you out like sheep among wolves. Therefore be as shrewd as snakes and as innocent as doves."

Christians need to be aware of what's going on, but they shouldn't give in to the practices of the world. Knowing God means you will suffer—just as Jesus did. That's part of the testimony of being a Christian. When you are different, people can see that you do love Jesus. I love being on the edge for the Lord!

Knowing God means you have a growing relationship with him. Sometimes he may seem far away, while other days he'll seem very near. While you struggle to know him, you'll grow. When it looks as if you don't have a friend to lean on, you'll turn to Jesus—and what you learn from him may influence you for the rest of your life. Grow with him! Don't give up on the best thing in life—your faith.

13

Living Inside a Family

If you've watched television in the past few years, you've gotten a lot of messages about family life. Probably you've come up with one of two ideas—either Dad always understands and Mom always supports, they laugh at troubles, and all is solved in half an hour, or it's every family member for himself, with Mom, Dad, and the kids going their own ways.

Perhaps you expect a home life like "The Cosby Show," with professional parents who still have time for the kids, a dad who can always second-guess what you need, and a mom who almost never yells. You know that's not real life, much as you may get some good laughs from the show. Dad can't easily package life when he comes home tired from a long day and has to deal with a stack of problems he doesn't have answers to. A bunch of television stars don't need discipline because they've messed up on something that could affect their futures.

Neither is life always the "I hate you" message given on other shows. Mom and Dad don't have to pick on each other, put each other down, and belittle the kids, too. That's a sign of a family life that isn't working.

People are different—and so are families. You can't use one cookie cutter to make the "perfect" family, though you can identify some ideas and actions that improve family life. *Communication, understanding,* and *love* build up a family, while belittling, condemnation, and criticism tear it down.

Let's take a look at four families. They are very different, but you may identify with one that will give you a handle on the type of life that's taking place in your home.

Sixteen-year-old Larry is good at sports, has lots of friends, and enjoys a good laugh. Usually he's in a good mood and is fun to be around. Even when others make mistakes, he doesn't put them down. Drugs, alcohol, pornography, and off-color jokes have no place in his life.

When I went to dinner with Larry and his family, I discovered why he's so much fun. His parents have given him a deep reservoir of love by their own example. They came from happy homes and love each other very much. They hug often and enjoy each other's company.

When we got to the restaurant, Larry held the door open for his mom, then helped her off with her coat. It was easy to see how proud he was of his parents.

Kids in Larry's school told me he's fortunate, and he knows it. He never takes his family for granted.

When I talked to Larry, he told me he worried about his looks a bit and where he would go to college, but for the most part he felt happy and content. Though he had wanted to become the football star, it hadn't happened. Instead, during his last few years of high school, he learned to focus on the fun he had with the guys. Now that his team will be broken up at the end of the year, he realizes how much he will miss those friendships with his teammates.

Larry has had good modeling from his parents. As a result, even when he does not make his goals, he can readjust them. Some days he may doubt himself, but he can hang in there. A good family life has given him a lot to draw on.

When I first made eye contact with Sharon, I was impressed with the way she didn't ignore others. As she passed other students or teachers in the hall, she said hello. The enthusiasm and self-confidence she exuded showed she liked herself.

Along with her younger brother and older sister, Sharon shares a home with her mom and step-dad. Her father died three years earlier, when she was in eighth grade.

Knowing how children often feel when a parent dies, I asked, "Didn't you feel as if your dad had abandoned you?"

"My mother and I got counseling for almost a year and a half after he died," Sharon shared. "I was able to grieve for him and even get angry that he had left me. But then I counted the good times we had. Mom and I realize that we will never be the same, yet we were fortunate to have him for as long as we did.

"I thought I'd never get over his loss, but I did. Today I feel great inside. Dad gave me a spark to live up to, and I have something to live for."

A couple of years after her husband's death, Sharon's mom met her step-father. During the waiting, Sharon's mother held onto her high morals, instead of grabbing the first available man. As a result, she has a husband who did not expect sex until they were married. He is gentle with Sharon, who can share her problems and pains with him.

Sharon is not dating anyone steadily, though she goes out with a couple of boys. She doesn't feel she needs to date someone to feel good about herself.

"I know that I will make it because of my mom and step-dad. My mom and I have never been closer, and I feel so near the Lord. I always wondered what good would come from my father's death, and now I know. I'm emotionally whole again and can help others who are going through the same situation."

Though Sharon's gone through tough times, she has her priorities straight, and life has become good for her again. She suffers through the normal insecurity of wondering where to go to college, and she's a bit of a perfectionist, but her self-esteem has become strong.

Don't let your self-esteem suffer when you face troubles. If pain is in your past, seek help and enjoy life again.

After Dan's mom saw me on television, she called me.

Her son was in trouble with the law, and she didn't know what to do. She told me that her husband had a job where he wasn't challenged. He spent most of his free time away from home and never bothered with the kids. "I feel as if I have to hold the family together all on my own," his wife cried.

Dan had refused counseling, but when he saw me on TV, he agreed to talk to me. Though I usually don't counsel people, I said I'd meet with Dan and his parents.

They seemed happy enough when we got together. But as we talked, I discovered that Dan's mom spent most of her time at the office. Because her family life was disappointing, she found value in her job and had gotten three promotions in a couple of years. The kids suffered because they rarely saw either parent.

Dan treated his parents well while I was there, but a couple of months later, I had to talk to him again. He had gotten into a fight at a bar, and the law had broken it up. His mom called me, since he wouldn't talk to anyone else.

Dan's anger poured out in the second conversation. "My parents don't love each other," he complained. "They never know what I do, either. Who cares if I get into a fight?"

When I shared this with his parents, Dan's dad refused to seek counseling, but his mother didn't. She is trying to make a better life for her three other children, because she doesn't want them to follow in Dan's footsteps.

When Dan responded to trouble, he did it the way he'd seen his father act—in anger. What was modeled in the home became his way of life. At seventeen, Dan can make a new start, if he will look for help. Instead of going to places that will get him into trouble, he needs to change his habits. Since his dad drinks, Dan needs to stay away from alcohol, unless he wants to become like his father. When he dates, he needs to be careful not to control the girl, or he may marry and abuse his wife.

Dan needs to look at his past and make new plans for the future if he wants a better life. He can do it.

When I met Susan, she was a high school sophomore who alternated between being very quiet and very loud and brassy. If she smiled—which didn't happen often— she had a pasted-on grin that didn't mean much.

Since then, Susan married. Recently I talked to her husband, and he told me the marriage was on the brink of disaster.

Her spending sprees and fear of sex caused Susan to get into counseling. There she found out that as a small child she had been sexually abused. Because she felt so bad, little Susan had repressed the memory—pushed it down so far that she didn't remember it. The rest of her family kept the secret that her dad was an alcoholic who abused his children. Only now, in her early twenties, is she beginning to deal with the problem.

Looking back, Susan can understand what happened. Her grandmother had been an alcoholic, and her dad followed in his mother's footsteps. Causing others pain made him feel good. Susan's mother wanted a man to take control of her life, and she feared her husband, so the children became victims.

Susan's husband, who came from a good family, loves her and wants to work things out. He agreed to go into therapy and counseling with her. They want to work through the past so they can share a happy future.

Can you relate to one of these families? Perhaps yours lies between two of them. The first two are healthy families, though both teens have their problems. For them, anxiety includes fears about their looks, reputation, dates, zits, and so on. The second two families are dysfunctional, and counseling may help them fill their reservoirs with love instead of pain.

If your family feels pain, get help today. You can have a better life if you invest in your future by learning how to end the hurt and start the healing.

14

What's It Like in My Family?

Now it's time to take a look at your own family. What makes you special or unhappy? Where have you done things right—or need to change? Take a careful look at the things that make your family special—or impossible.

In the following pages, as you read about the habits of healthy and dysfunctional families, keep in mind that we're looking at your family so intently because your home is your greatest practice field, and it has a strong influence on your self-esteem. Because the way you view yourself is so important to your life, it's worth taking stock of where you've come from, even if it hurts a bit. If you don't find many positive elements in your family, remember, that can change, with God's help. Keep reading, and your effort may pay big dividends for the rest of your life.

What Makes a Family Healthy?

In order to identify a good family life, we'll take a look at some of the common elements that are part of the happy family. Be warned—no family has all of these, and I've seen few families that have most of them, though they *are* out there. Even unhealthy families can become positive, happy, and loving. Many of the tips you'll need are in this book.

How many of these qualities are in your home?

1. Parents spend a lot of time with the family. Mom and Dad do not look for ways to spend nights out with others or avoid coming home. They like their homelife, so they spend lots of time with the family. It is so important to them that they make it a priority in their lives.

I'm not saying parents never have special times to themselves—like a date night—but they love their home and kids.

2. Family members give one another attention. Mom, Dad, and the children pay close attention to one another. When one has a concern, they all take part. Maybe they will listen carefully, give some advice, or lend a hand with a project. Because they care for one another this way, they build family respect.

3. They share love. Healthy families exhibit love. We're not talking about abnormal, pride-filled conceit, but a self-giving love, the kind Jesus talked about when he told us to love our neighbors as we love ourselves.

4. Parents show their love for each other. Mom and Dad enjoy each other and are friends. They want to share each other's company. In a blended family, the step-parent will love his or her spouse. Single parents will be content alone or with friends and enjoy life. They enjoy the things they do and are proud to have God watch their actions, because they know what they do pleases him.

5. Parents communicate on an intimate level. Conversation is not limited to the weather and other "safe" topics. Mom and Dad can talk about anything at any time, because each is concerned about the other. Even when one wants to discuss something that does not greatly interest the other, they will communicate on that subject. If something is important to a person you love, you will listen.

6. *Parents communicate openly and often with children.* Communication lines are open between parents and children. When a teen feels angry with his dad, he can say that in a normal and loving way. A disappointed parent can tell a child why she feels hurt. "I'm sorry," "You hurt my feelings," "I love you," "I need you," and, "Why didn't you listen yesterday, when I really needed you?" are all phrases that can be spoken in a normal family.

7. *No one walks on eggshells.* Have you ever felt as if you could not say something to a family member, had to watch out for someone's temper, or felt fear that you might be harmed? All these can make you feel as if you have to walk on eggshells. Can you be yourself, or do you feel as if you have to perform just right before you'll be accepted? When you don't have to worry, you have a healthy family pattern.

8. *Parents date each other.* When I first met my wife, Holly, we dated all the time. Once we got married, we still went out a lot; but when the kids came, we stopped for a while. All our attention focused on them. Today we've reinstated a date night. Every few months we go away for a weekend together. Dating keeps our love alive and vital. People who don't set aside time for their spouses take them for granted and drift apart.

9. *Families truly listen to one another.* You may hear a person's words, but have you truly listened? Do you know what caused him to hurt, how she managed to build a winning situation, or what plans he has for the future? A good listener knows what's behind the words. Families that share one another's good points, bad points, hurts, and excitement have good communication habits.

10. They avoid verbal, emotional, or physical abuse. Healthy families have normal touches and hugs. Parents do not abuse their children by beating them, grabbing them and shaking them, or otherwise physically harming them. They do not strike out at one another with put-downs. (As my daughter Crystal says, "If you can't say something nice, don't say anything at all.") Instead they verbally lift others up.

Your family may lose patience with you and say something wrong on occasion. Don't give up and cry that you're abused. When it becomes a habit or it happens so strongly that mental scars begin to show, however, you need to deal with it. How people speak to you can have an impact on how you feel about yourself.

11. Families solve difficulties. When you have a problem, can you talk to your parents? When you feel pain or have a situation you can't find an answer for, can you ask Mom or Dad for wise counsel? Healthy, loving families care for the problems of others in the family. They are there for a hurting member and help solve problems.

12. Families express and receive affection. Can you easily give a hug if you need one? Do others offer them when you hurt? Can Mom and Dad say, "I love you"? Healthy families regularly share their feelings and receive love back.

13. People value one another. Even when your brother and sister haven't made straight As, gotten on the team, or been voted into a good position, do you love them? Do they love you, too, for who you are? Because they love, family members will treat one another as important, special people.

14. They feel a sense of family pride. Do you feel honored to be in your family? Do you brag about the people you live with and feel good about them? You don't always have to agree with your whole family in order to feel family pride. If you need some pride, work at it. Like an athlete, you'll need to practice to develop those family-pride muscles.

15. Families make joint decisions. You'll feel free to give your opinion in a healthy home. Before your family buys a car or goes on vacation, you'll know about it and have a chance to share your thoughts. Your parents and siblings want your advice and want to discover how you feel about it.

16. Shame does not ruin the value of a family member. Recently, at a funeral, I heard a son tell of his pride in his mother. He loved to bring home friends to meet her. Family members work to make one another proud of them. They have nothing to regret, because they live out positive character qualities.

17. Families work through stress together. All families have problems, but healthy ones work through them together. They care and share enough to find the solutions that take them beyond the pain. Each person's stress is considered by others. They do not try to add to the problems, but to find answers.

18. Family members grieve with one another. Healthy families encourage one another to work through losses, whether the cat disappears or Grandma dies. When you feel sad, you're sad, and they recognize that. They give one another plenty of time to cry, hurt, and express feelings. Healthy families never pass on messages such as, "Don't cry, it's over." Instead they say, "Okay, it's normal. Cry about it and get it out. We will hurt together."

19. When they hurt others, they ask for forgiveness. Healthy families have lots of people who can say, "I goofed up," "Please forgive me," "I'm sorry," or, "I care about you, and I'm sorry I hurt you."

20. Parents support children's activities and ideas. When you play baseball, is your dad the only one in the stands? Has your mother come to a recital or play that you took part in? Healthy families show up for one another's activities. They help with homework and give encouragement when a member has to memorize Bible verses for church or lines for a school play. Whatever goals and dreams you have, your family takes part in them.

21. Family meetings. Healthy families get together to talk. They may pray together, share their feelings on a certain subject, or discuss a problem they all face. Instead of waiting for a fight, they talk things out in an orderly, loving way. Because they keep up on everyone's needs, no one has to worry about volume control.

22. Parents are good neighbors. Healthy families share with others. They meet people and invite them to their home. They have good relationships with people around them.

23. Parents have their own hobbies and interests. Mom and Dad don't become obsessed with a hobby, but they do keep up their own interests. They have activities they enjoy and look forward to. I play tennis when my children are in school or in bed. On Saturdays, when I play with my travel team, my family comes to support me. If I didn't do this, a creative part of me would remain unfulfilled.

24. Children have one-on-one time with parents. Just as parents spend time together, so do parents and children. Maybe they go to a special restaurant or spend Saturday morning with one child. My brother takes each of his children to one special restaurant, where they try to get a favorite booth. During the time together, they grow close and communicate well.

25. Parents are in control of money. Do your parents have a savings account? Do they keep good track of their money, instead of overspending? Healthy families keep control of their finances. When they want things, they make sure they can pay for them before they pull out the credit card. Even better, they may pay cash. Some teens get whatever they want from their parents, but they never learn to earn money and save it. When we can't control money, we can't control our lives.

26. Parents plan for the future. Have your parents set aside some money for your education? Instead of buying things today that they will regret tomorrow, they should provide security by thinking about what's ahead that they will need. From them you can learn to plan for the future.

27. The family is exciting. Can you laugh easily and share a good joke? Are you spontaneous? Can you go out for Chinese food on the spur of the moment? Do you suddenly grab your coats and head for a friend's house, to watch a good video?

Place a check by each of these qualities that are part of your family. If you found 15 or more, you are in really good shape. Where you miss one, it could just be that your parents don't do it, and all is fine—or it could be a negative point in your family. For instance, you may not have regular family meetings, but you may talk about problems while you're traveling in the car or eating dinner. You've found a different way of doing the same thing, though you might not name it a family meeting. Don't penalize yourself for that, but work on the negative points you have identified.

Unhealthy Family Traits

Just as healthy families have certain habits, unhealthy ones often make consistent—and often correctable— mistakes. Do you see these in your family?

1. A lack of love between parents. Remember, your parents set the tone for your family. Morale will filter down from the top—you can't raise it from the bottom very well. If your parents don't like each other or never express their love for each other, you will also have a hard time expressing love. Why? Because if you never see it in your family, you don't know how to show other people you care by kind words and actions. When all you've seen is fights and harsh words, you have trouble knowing how to act. Imagine if someone asked you to learn trigonometry by yourself. You'd have trouble, wouldn't you? It's the same with family life. When someone shows you how it works best, it's easiest to pick it up.

2. Abuse. A physically abused child is beaten; a sexually abused one has a parent who uses her for his own pleasure; verbal abuse exists when parents always yell and tell their child he's no good. Emotional abuse may occur when a parent so leans on a child for love that he can never go out and have normal friendships.

Abuse destroys the family structure and must be stopped.

3. Parents fight. Do your parents argue or fight a lot? Do they often act mad at each other, raise their voices in anger, or even hit each other? This is not a normal situation.

4. Workaholics. Do your parents spend so much time on the job that you never see them? Does Dad come home so tired that he can't do anything with the family, or does he stay so tuned into work that you can't get a thought in edgewise? If so, after a while, you won't ask his advice on anything, because he's so obsessed with his job.

Maybe your mom spends so much time doing volunteer work that she doesn't have time for the family. Whether or not they get paid for it, parents may become so bound up in what they do that they ignore family needs.

5. Alcoholism. Do either of your parents have an addiction to alcohol? You don't have to be a bum in the street to be an alcoholic. Parents who regularly drink to enjoy life or avoid trouble may be alcoholics.

You may have sensed it but don't dare mention it out loud. If you fear telling your parents and have to walk on eggshells, you probably do have an alcoholic parent.

6. *Drug use.* Alcohol is the number-one drug that destroys families, but your parents may use crack, marijuana, or prescription drugs to ease the pain of life. Do you see it in your family?

7. *Rage-aholic.* Does either of your parents get angry easily and go through the roof? When this becomes a pattern of family life, it spells trouble. Sometimes physical or verbal abuse results.

8. *Affairs.* Does either of your parents seem to be having an affair? Maybe you cannot prove it but have suspected it for some time. If Mom or Dad has a secret love, your family is in pain—and you will carry part of that hurt.

9. *Lack of positive emotions.* Is Mom or Dad depressed? Can they rarely show excitement for life? Do they simply put up with life, instead of enjoying it? If so, you need to realize that you can get excited about life. You can shed the hurts that have influenced you and start again.

10. *Disappointment with life.* Have your parents made it clear that they didn't marry the person they wanted to, didn't get the job they wanted, or wish they'd never had children? Such people are disappointed with life. Their morale will influence you.

11. *Denial.* Do your parents avoid problems by saying they don't exist? Do they say they don't have a drinking problem, when they have to drink all weekend to enjoy themselves? Do they tell you you were not abused sexually, when your emotional scars show it happened? Do they deny that they pressure you too heavily to get good grades and earn a scholarship? Many dysfunctional families will not admit that a problem exists.

12. Lack of love in childhood. Did your mom and dad have healthy homes when they were young? Was your mother filled with love? If not, she has little love to pass on to you. Did Dad try to fill his heart with love by going into marriage—but it hasn't worked?

13. Lack of parent-child communication. Is it nearly impossible for you to share anything with your parents? Have you learned to keep things inside or just talk to your friends, because communication with Mom and Dad is blocked? Perhaps you talk to a teacher or counselor instead.

If your parents are so preoccupied that you cannot talk to them, your family needs help. Get the special attention that will make your family well.

14. Eggshell syndrome. Do you have to walk on eggshells around your parents? Does constant anger between your mother and sister cause everyone to fear saying a word? Does your father show he's jealous of your brother's success? Does your mother feel angry because she "wasted her life" raising children? I call this eggshell syndrome, because you have to step so lightly around your family members.

15. No encouragement to get along with brothers and sisters. A certain amount of rivalry between siblings is normal. When one gets attention because he has done well and the other doesn't feel special, that unspecial child may feel bad. But when parents never confront the situation and end it, it may grow.

My own family did not encourage me to get along with my younger brother, who was better than me at sports and using his hands. I discouraged him from playing with me and my friends, because I didn't want Dale to show me up. If I could do something to make him feel bad, it made me feel good. Because my parents had their own problems, they never encouraged me to talk about how I felt. They didn't show me how glad I should be to have a brother by letting me visit with an only child. A normal family encourages unity between siblings.

16. Parents overspend. Spendaholics who max out their credit cards and have tremendous problems because of anxiety and a lack of money have a dysfunctional family life. When all you can do is worry about money, you can't have a happy family.

17. Extremes are normal. Families that don't know how to love seem filled with extremes. They may take part in compulsive behavior—food binges, overspending by buying larger houses or cars, and so on—and the children will think that it's normal, because they only knew that. Healthy self-images do not result from this kind of extremism.

18. Worries fill the house. Does one of your parents worry all the time? Are Mom and Dad depressed or filled with fear? Do they withdraw from life when they feel this way? If so, they need to seek help. If you begin to see that you worry all the time or set yourself very high goals so that you overachieve, you have been influenced by your homelife.

19. Parents instill guilt and shame in children. No one needs to go to school to learn guilt and shame. They come easily to us. Sometimes we sin, know that it is wrong, and feel ashamed. That is healthy, since it may keep us from making the same mistake twice. On the other hand, parents who make their children feel as if they can never live up to their expectations, cannot take care of Mom and Dad, or do not worry about the "right" things have passed on unhealthy messages.

20. You feel ashamed of your family. Do you never want to be seen in public with your family? Probably you feel deep shame about them or know that your family takes part in "secret" activities that you cannot share with anyone. No one may have told you not to tell, but you understand that there is a "quiet rule" in your house.

21. You handle all your own problems. Others in your family are not resources for you when you face trouble. This is not normal, but it can be changed, if you seek the right help.

22. You cannot grieve for losses. Recently I met a girl who was breaking apart because she could not grieve for her grandmother. After her death, the girl's mom said, "She had a long, full life; stop crying!" The teen never knew that she was reacting normally to the loss, and she felt guilt and shame.

23. Parents obsessed with family. This is about as bad as parents who ignore their families. Occasionally families go to the other extreme, where the kids can't stay at a grandparent's house, because no one is good enough for them. In order to spend all their time with their children, the parents avoid hobbies and friendships. Mom and Dad don't even take time off for themselves. Everyone needs some breathing room. Without some space sometime, the family becomes unbalanced.

Check off the things that fit your family. If several of these are in your home, you may need more help than this book. Even one may ruin your life. Talk to an older, wiser person—a Christian counselor, if possible. Get the help you need.

Review Your Family

Take a look at your family. Where has it made mistakes? Take heart, for you need not live with that error. If your parents just got a divorce or your father is an alcoholic, don't blame yourself. Instead look at what mistakes you made and how you can do better. Only take responsibility for what *you* can change.

Now look at what was good in your family. Did you have a close family? Did your dad share a hobby with you? Look for the big things and the not-so-noticeable ones. Did your dad spend hours teaching you to play football? Did your mom show you how to cook—or do the laundry? Make certain your view of family life is not one-sided. Even dysfunctional families do some things right.

Family-Life Review

1. List fun times you remember in your family. What did you do? Who was there? Did you do the same activities many times?
2. List times of trouble you remember. What hurt you most about them? Do you still feel the pain of that memory, or have things gotten better?
3. Do you remember sharing special times with your family members? List each. Did you do them regularly?
4. What do you wish your family had done together that you didn't do? What held you back?

Once you've taken a look at your family, through the exercises in this chapter, don't give up. Recently I took a test like the first one and learned that my family life as a child had not been as perfect as I'd fooled myself into believing it was. Even though I didn't know about all that was going on—I've since learned more from my family—it rubbed off on me. A child in any house gets part of the love—or pain—that is in that household. Even though he or she may not personally experience abuse, if it's in the family, it will show up in scars that may take many years to appear. Healing is not an easy process, but it can happen.

If you have felt pain, get through it by identifying it, grieving over it, getting through the anger, and moving beyond it. A caring counselor can help you through the process.

I'm with you on this. How I wish I could jump through the pages of this book and tell you how much I care. If I could show you how much God cares, too, I would. Get the help you need, and you will feel much happier. Don't deny your pain or wonder why you hate certain types of people—the opposite sex, authority figures, or someone else.

Avoiding the pain now may seem easier, but the hurt will keep coming back if you don't take courage and start to change. Won't it be worth it to sleep well at night, express how you feel to others, and have the ability to say yes to the right things God tells you to do?

By reading this book, you've come a long way. Hang in there. The journey is getting exciting, and I know you can finish the race!

15

Mean-What-You-Say Communication

A little while ago, I almost lost a long-term friendship because my friend and I both thought we had a one-way relationship. While I felt I always had to call him, he felt he initiated things more. We seemed caught in a trap.

I felt embarrassed to admit that I needed my friend and that his friendship was important to me—but I'm so glad I did. When I told him, he agreed with me. "I need it, too, but. . . ." He began to detail past troubles that he'd never admitted bothered him. All this time he'd hidden the anger he felt.

"Hold on, I have hurts, too," I said, and as I told him my side, he expressed surprise that I had held the pain so deep inside.

Our long friendship, which had brought our families together for fun times, almost ended because the two of us had not communicated clearly about how we felt. We saved that friendship by crying and yelling and becoming honest with each other. Most of all, we shared our words and feelings—we communicated.

To have good friendships and family lives—a positive social life—we need to be able to communicate clearly and deeply. Let's look at some practical tips for relating well to people at home, at school, and in our communities.

Let's Talk About Talk

Talk—that's what communication is really about, isn't it?

No!

Listening is the greatest communication skill you can learn. To really hear another, you must understand what a person says, feels, and means. It requires that you put aside your own ideas temporarily, accept that person as being important, and give of yourself. If you don't do these things, you might be hearing, but you have not listened.

When you talk to a friend, teacher, or parent, who is more important—you or that other person? Do you fight to get in your next sentence, or do you tune in to what's going into your ears? Do you take that person's words to heart, or are you too busy thinking about how you plan to respond or what she will think about your next sentence?

The Bible has some attitude advice for people who want to communicate clearly:

> *Philippians 2:3 (TLB):* "Don't be selfish; don't live to make a good impression on others. Be humble, thinking of others as better than yourself."

True listening requires that you put that person first for a while and treat him with true respect.

Well, no one else does that for me, you may be thinking. The Bible also warns:

Romans 12:2 (TLB): "Don't copy the behavior and customs of this world, but be a new and different person with a fresh newness in all you do and think. . . ."

You don't have to respond the way the world does by implying to people that they are not important enough to get a hearing. Putting yourself on a communication pedestal that way shows you feel that only your own words have importance.

Start to listen to others, and you will often discover that they begin to spend more time asking about your concerns. Address their deepest concerns, and they are more likely to hear yours.

Talk That Listens

Does communicating well mean you never open your mouth? Of course not; but it does mean that when you speak you do so wisely, following this advice:

Ephesians 4:29 (TLB): "Don't use bad language. Say only what is good and helpful to those you are talking to, and what will give them a blessing."

That verse gives us two good communication rules:

1. Say only wholesome words and phrases. Have you noticed how popular the put-down is? Can you get through a day without hearing one? It's easy to find fault with others, but the Bible says it's not wise.

Instead, only say the things about another that you would say in front of Jesus. That eliminates the "Guess what I heard about So-and-So" type of conversation and replaces it with something better.

2. Edify others. To edify someone means you build him up, instead of tearing him down. Before you unload on your friend, consider what it will mean to her. Will it ruin her day for no good reason? Will it help her with a problem she faces?

Do you lift up others or wipe them out with your words? Do you have good conversational habits, or do you need to develop new ones? Take the Communication Quiz to find out.

Communication Quiz

__   1. I share my feelings with others.
__   2. I talk openly and honestly with people.
__   3. In general, I try to trust people and look for the best in them.
__   4. When others talk, I look directly in their eyes and really tune in to what they say.
__   5. If I don't understand what someone means, I politely ask questions.
__   6. I'm aware of nonverbal communication in others. (If they look angry, fold their arms, seem bored, or act depressed.)
__   7. I try to be sensitive to others' feelings.
__   8. I always take into account the speaker's background and age.
__   9. I look carefully at the facts when I communicate.
__ 10. I'm positive by nature.
__ 11. If someone smiles or laughs at what I say, I feel good inside.
__ 12. I pray for others on a regular basis.
__ 13. Being a supportive friend or servant is important to me.
__ 14. If others disagree with my ideas, I try to learn from their point of view.

Did you check most of these? If so, you are an effective communicator. Did you find some places to improve on? Then know that you can learn better communication techniques.

Check off the following traits that are part of your communication.

__ 1. I hold my feelings inside. I figure that close friends should just know how I feel.
__ 2. I'm quiet, and it's hard for me to share with others.
__ 3. I have trouble trusting people. There are a lot of creeps out there.
__ 4. I try to do most of the talking when I communicate with others.
__ 5. It's easy for me to forget people's names, even moments after we've met.
__ 6. When I talk with others, I look around the room from time to time, to see who's there.
__ 7. If someone is hurting inside, I figure it's her problem. Besides, what could I do anyway?
__ 8. It's easy for me to be negative and pessimistic.
__ 9. If someone smiles as I walk by, I think he is laughing at me.
__ 10. I've got too many problems of my own to worry about helping others.
__ 11. I wonder why people don't like me or wait on me more than they do.
__ 12. I easily get angry if others disagree with me.

If you checked most of these, you have some poor communication habits.

Did you see a pattern to your problems? Perhaps you:

- Are too busy thinking about yourself to communicate well
- Think negatively about others and want to avoid them
- Fear people, because they might harm you
- Don't want to become involved with people

Much of your happiness in life will depend on how well you interact with others. If you fear people, ignore them, or can't be bothered with them, you have formed some poor habits that may harm you for life. Relationships with friends, your spouse, and employers will deeply depend on your skill in hearing what they mean and telling them your own thoughts. So begin to practice caring for others today.

Communication Obstacles

Communication is a learned skill that you can work on. After you have talked to someone, maybe you need to review what went on. Did you make some of the communication mistakes listed above, or did you show the positive communication methods? Were you blocked by some of the following common communication obstacles?

1. Disagreement between words and actions. Do your words and actions agree, or do you say one thing and do another?

From the letters I've received about date rapes, I know that sometimes they happen when communication is not consistent. For example, when it's 3:00 A.M., a couple has been drinking and dancing for hours, and they end up in his place, trouble is waiting to happen. A woman who lies naked on a bed and says no has little credibility.

I'm not suggesting that a man ever has an excuse for rape, but when words and actions disagree, the stage is set for something to go wrong.

To communicate clearly, check that you are not giving a hidden message. Your mind might be going in one direction, and your emotions in another; that will cause confusion for the listener. It can cause problems, even in a situation much less devastating than a date rape. Make every effort to think and speak clearly.

2. Too much noise. If you are talking to your friend while the music is blasting, he might not hear or understand. Don't ask your parents a question when they are deeply involved in an intense movie. Outside noise like this does not aid good communication.

You also have inside noise from the hurts, thoughts, and preoccupations in your mind and heart. While you feel distracted by them, you do not communicate well. Leave your inside noise at home for a time while you listen. If you suspect that inside noise interferes from the other person's side, discover what it is, so that clear communication can begin.

3. Too much or too little space. Did you know that how well you hear may be influenced by how close a person stands to you? People have natural assumptions that go with distance.

For example, if a person you've just met stands in your face, you probably try to back away. You don't know him well enough to feel comfortable that close up. If your dad yells, "I love you," from across the room, when you're really hurting, it won't have the same impact as if he stands next to you and puts an arm around your shoulders and says the same words. How close or near people are does communicate a message.

Here's a rule of thumb about distance for most Americans (other nationalities may differ):

Public distance: Stay ten to fourteen feet from a public audience.

Social distance: Stay four to six feet from others at a business meeting.

Personal distance: A distance of one to two-and-a-half feet is appropriate when you talk to casual acquaintances.

Intimate distance: You can get up to eighteen inches from close friends and family.

4. Inconsistent tone of voice. Has anyone yelled, "I said I wasn't mad, didn't I?" at you? Did you believe what she said? Her tone said much more than her words. Or maybe someone told you, "Okay, I forgive you. Now I don't want to hear any more about it," in a hurt tone of voice. You didn't believe his hurt was over and that he'd forgiven you, did you?

When you say things you don't mean, your tone of voice may give you away. Watch what you really mean, and say it in a tone of voice that backs it up, or don't say it at all. Become aware of what people really mean when they act this way, and talk things out, if you think they are not saying what's in their hearts.

5. *Slang that confuses.* Mary and Judy had a confusing conversation.

Mary: "Sue's parents are strange."

Judy: "You mean they're weird."

Mary: "No, just strange. They really act weird sometimes, but not weird-weird—if you know what I mean."

Judy: "I'm sorry, I *don't* know what you mean. Do you like them?"

Mary: "What do you think? They act like kids. I went to their house, and the dad, well, he is so hyper, and he was telling the strangest jokes I've ever heard. And the mom acts like a sixteen-year-old."

Judy: "Boy, I'm never going there."

Mary: "Why not? They're neat parents. My mom's a lawyer. She's so stuffy and boring. Not Sue's parents. They come to all her games and work with the church youth group. I wish mine cared as much about what I do and acted so good with my friends."

Judy: "Boy, this talk sure was strange. I'm glad you say what you mean and mean what you say—you know what I mean?"

Judy felt glad when that conversation ended (and so did I). Mary took the word *strange* and gave it her own definition and she seemed to be inconsistent in her ideas. If she's always so confusing to talk to, can you see why others might avoid her or simply call her—you guessed it!—strange?

The same goes with the slang you hear in school. Does your mom know what *bad* means in your world, or will you confuse her when you use the word? Clear communication requires that each person understands the definition of a word and that ideas be presented clearly.

Miscommunication causes trouble in marriages, business situations, and churches. When you don't know what others think, how they feel, and why they made a critical decision, you cannot clearly identify problems and their solutions.

Good communication opens people up, allows them to grow closer, and lets them feel good about themselves. Spend time discovering your own communication style. Develop clearer ways of speaking and writing. You'll see changes in your life and in your self-esteem.

16

Looking Good, Feeling Good

People like to look good—and let's face it, when you look good you usually have a better chance for success in America. Teachers pay more attention to the best-dressed, handsome, and neat teens. Advertising tells us how important it is to be pretty.

So what do you do if you won't win any beauty prizes or can't afford a great wardrobe? Do you give up on life? Can you never look and feel good? No!

A Different Perspective

How can we get away from these harsh look-good rules that come from the world? By seeing what God has to say about how we look.

Romans 12:2 (TLB): "Don't copy the behavior and customs of this world, but be a new and different person with a fresh newness in all you do and think. Then you will learn from your own experience how his ways will really satisfy you."

1 Peter 3:3, 4 (TLB): "Don't be concerned about the out-ward beauty that depends on jewelry, or beautiful clothes, or hair arrangement. Be beautiful inside, in your hearts, with the lasting charm of a gentle and quiet spirit which is so precious to God."

Proverbs 31:30 (TLB): "Charm can be deceptive and beauty doesn't last, but a woman who fears and reverences God shall be greatly praised."

Psalm 147:10, 11 (TLB): "The speed of a horse is nothing to him [God]. How puny in his sight is the strength of a man. But his joy is in those who reverence him, those who expect him to be loving and kind."

Getting caught up in your biceps or your wardrobe won't make you—or God—happy. God knows our souls will last longer than our new Reeboks. Inside stuff is better than outside stuff. Our hearts, souls, and characters last forever. So he places importance on the inside stuff.

Look your best, but don't put your faith in that. Have balance between your inside and outside qualities.

Develop Inner Beauty

You can look good on the outside by spending a few minutes fixing your hair, changing your clothes, or putting on new shoes, but how about inner beauty? Is there a quick fix for that? No. Honesty, love for God and others, respect, integrity, and trustworthiness take time to build. You cannot develop them overnight, but they last, once you've put them into your life.

Jesus says that you can take one of two roads—the wide one, which gives you lots of company, but few real friends, or the narrow, challenging one that ends in an eternal friendship with him. Which will you choose?

I became a public speaker because I love the chal-lenge of doing something most people fear—talking to a live audience. Most folks don't want to get up in front of others and say even a few words, but I like it. To me, it doesn't matter that public speaking isn't popular with a lot of people. I don't need to decide on my career based on their opinions. But it wasn't always that way with me.

For twenty-eight years I did what everyone else did. When they sinned, I sinned. When they yelled, I did, too. When they drank, I went along with the crowd. Why did I do the things I hated? Because I wanted other people to like me. That was the only way I knew to get their attention.

My response was not healthy, though I didn't realize it then.

Are you in the place I was in twenty-eight years ago? Then you've got some work to do. Like me, you've tried to feel good based on your outer beauty, not your inner strengths. Living that way will lead to a lot of heartache.

Why do I have to change today? you may ask. *Can't I just have fun now and do all that when I'm older?*

If you put it off, when you are married and have children the changes will be harder. They'll involve other people. When you have to put right mistakes you've made with your family, it will not be easy. Save yourself trouble by doing the work before you hit college or have a career.

The Blessing of Inner Beauty

When I met my wife, Holly, her outer beauty attracted me—but I also felt the attractions of other women, too. I'd date other women, but somehow I always ended up dumping them and getting together with Holly again. Why? Because she has a special inner beauty. She loves people and knows how to listen. She encourages me and likes to hear about my fears and joys. Even when I'm not perfect, she cares about me. Because she loves me so much, she doesn't care that I'm not perfect. When she goes along with what I want to do, she makes it easy for me to go along with her plans. If I have something very important going on, she may cancel her important plans, because she truly likes to see me happy.

Since my family life was not the greatest, I grew up with low self-esteem, which meant I had a low self-worth. When people noticed and talked about me, I felt important. But Holly doesn't need acclaim to feel good about herself. Most of the time, she's on an even keel. Others try to gossip to her, saying, "Do you want to hear about this?" but she says, "No!"

I'm not claiming Holly is perfect, but she has so many inner strengths that her face glows with them. I've never known someone who was mad at her or held a grudge against my wife. In fact, several people (including my brother) have told me they wanted wives like Holly.

When they said that, they didn't mean they wanted a woman who was five feet, ten inches tall; they were admiring her inner beauty. Her character and integrity caught their eyes.

You may have had a rough family life or problems along the way, but you can develop your inner beauty, too, by using the guidelines in this book.

When you look at people, see their inside qualities that make them beautiful, too. That way you won't be as likely to fall in love with someone who only looks good on the outside (we call that lust, not love). Put your values where God does, and you will be more successful. Of course you'll like yourself much better, too.

Seek the Truth

We've come a long way in our search for a very happy, contented you. Perhaps you see a lot of room for growth in your life. Maybe you feel as if you could never accomplish it all.

Remember, inch by inch, it's a cinch. Don't take on your whole world at once. Instead pick a small portion to start on. Maybe you need to contact a counselor. So focus on that first. Counseling may help you find the truth you need.

Whether or not you seek professional help, find the truth and pursue it. Only truth will set you free. Once you find the truth, follow these steps:

1. *Confront it honestly.* You may need help to see through the denial in your life. Maybe you've avoided a problem by pretending it didn't exist or by losing yourself in depression, or maybe your mind did it for you by forgetting the hurt you could not deal with. Whatever protection you've created, you'll have to go beyond that to see what is real.

2. *Don't quit.* The "easy" route might be to give up, but problems don't often disappear completely. When you push it all in a closet, the closet only becomes fuller and fuller, until one day you can't close the door, and it spills out into your room. Quitters won't improve their lives—they'll only put off the problem until it's bigger and nastier.

I know what it's like to hurt. My dad had a drinking problem, and he wanted to control people. Our family avoided the problem for years, but like a dead elephant in the middle of the room, we could only walk around it. Everyone knew the problem was there. For years I was the great pretender, the positive thinker who believed his family had been wonderful.

Only since my dad died has the truth come out. I didn't remember a lot of the trouble and pain in the family, but my mom did. Now we are dealing with it, and for the first time in my life, I am learning to look honestly at my life. Never before have I felt such peace.

I've learned that I don't have to do things to look good to people. The outer things—what I wear, how well I speak, and so on are not as important as who I am inside. God's view of me is more important than trying to make someone think I'm a hotshot.

Potter and Clay

We all know who made us, don't we?

Isaiah 64:8 (TLB): "And yet, O Lord, you are our Father. We are the clay and you are the Potter. We are all formed by your hand."

Do you remember playing with Legos or Tinker Toys as a child? You were wiser than the building blocks, when you designed a house, a figure, or something else. You had an idea about where you were going when you built—and the blocks didn't have a say in what they wanted to be.

It's the same with God and us. He created us and has great plans. We can love, have feelings, laugh, cry, know right from wrong, and have the capacity to make good choices.

Parents and situations around us may have a part in our molding. A child may lose his mom and dad while he's an infant, and adoptive parents or an orphanage may take him in. What he experiences there will touch his life. Or the family you were born into may be shattered by illness, abuse, or divorce.

The pot seems cracked or shattered, but you are still there, confused. What can you do?

Realize that you are not stuck with a "cracked pot." You can change yourself by changing your thinking, and you will feel differently about yourself. As a result, your actions will change. Again and again show yourself that you love yourself, and your self-worth will rise.

Let God help you remold yourself. You want to be made in the image of Jesus Christ, not some old, cracked pot. When you think about yourself, focus on these truths:

- God's definition of what you should be is different from the world's definition.
- God wants you to know that your uniqueness plus your relationship with him equals a healthy self-esteem.
- Sin carries legitimate guilt for the person who committed it.
- If you ask for forgiveness and truly mean it in your heart, God will grant it.
- If you choose to hold on to guilt after you receive forgiveness, it is your fault.
- If God approves of your character, you don't need to have the world's approval.

The world will give you messages that tear you down. Compare these to God's messages, above:

- The world says you should concentrate on outside looks.
- It wants you to focus on your weaknesses, instead of your strong points.
- If you make a mistake, it wants you to wallow in it instead of accepting the fact that everyone goofs up, and we learn from mistakes.

How can you change? By rerouting your thinking. Here are some guidelines.

Thought-Changing Techniques

1. Realize that thoughts influence emotions. Change your thoughts, and your emotions will change, too.
2. Begin by identifying your thought patterns. Once you have done that, you may realize that your feelings and emotions are triggered by certain thoughts.

   3. Identify faulty thoughts and challenge them. When erroneous ones come into your mind, argue with them.
   4. Recognize that you don't respond to what happens to you—you respond to the way you think or interpret the situation.
   5. Understand that the truth will set you free if you confront it and stick to the process.
   6. You can feel great about yourself because you are pursuing the truth.
   7. When you feel uncomfortable with the truth about the past, remember that, though it makes the present uncomfortable, it will help you in the future.
   8. Subconsciously you may still receive negative messages. Identify the underlying reasons for what you do, and you can change them.
   9. Old thought patterns take time to change. Be patient with yourself as you confront and try to alter them.
   10. Changing your thoughts will not come naturally to you. It takes hard work.
   11. Peace can come to you when you pursue the truth. It's as if you were learning to play "Chopsticks." At first the lessons on the piano are slow and hard, but one day a whole orchestra will play peace in your heart.
   12. Like learning to drive, thought changing takes much practice. Surprisingly, one day it will seem second nature. You can feel great about yourself in a godly way, if you persist.
   13. Keep looking for slow improvement. This is not an overnight process, but an ongoing change.
   14. Learn from your mistakes, don't wallow in them.

Really Looking Good

By now I hope you realize that, when you only try to look good on the outside, the sole person you fool is yourself. Dressing in the best clothes, wearing perfume or aftershave, or taking regular showers is simply part of what it means to look good, because you cannot get away from yourself.

To look really good, you have to feel good about yourself. By that I don't mean you have to be perfect—no one is. People who expect that they will never make mistakes set themselves up for a lifetime of disappointment. You need to have God's view of you and be working on your own inside beauty.

When she was in the sixth grade, everyone noticed Denise. She had the best wardrobe of anyone, and the boys paid attention to her. Girls tried to be around her and copied her stylish dressing and conversation. Her grades were good, too. A few years later, in high school, she no longer stood out much. Lots of other girls dressed just as well, and her grades no longer made her special. Achievement had dropped, in favor of her social life. To feel good about herself, she had to have people complimenting her looks, her personality, and her attractiveness to boys. Denise never knew that God judged her differently—that she didn't have to compete with the other girls in the class to be loved. She had gotten unbalanced, because she spent all her time in the social corner of her life.

You'll need to spend time on all four corners of your foundation to do more than look good on the outside. Grow mentally and physically, but also spend time with God and your family. A lopsided foundation means you have a lopsided building. The stress that creates will make cracked walls, an uneven ceiling, and a roof that's angled as if it would fall to pieces any minute. In your life, it shows up as dissatisfaction, fear, and confusion— low self-esteem.

Feeling good will make you look good, too. Once you know God and others love you, despite your flaws, you will be able to look people in the eye, reach out to those who hurt, and encourage everyone you meet. Whether you wear the latest fashions or just look neat and clean, people will be attracted to you. No one can resist a person who truly cares. Make that your goal, and you will look good and feel good inside!

That's the healthy self-esteem God and I want so very much for you. Don't forget, you were made in his image, slightly less than the angels who guard you.

God has a plan for your life. Search out the truth about you and him: These truths will set you free to accept yourself and the salvation he offers. When you commit yourself to living for Jesus, he will forgive your past and live in your heart. Your future—heaven—will be guaranteed. Why *shouldn't* you like yourself?

If this book has touched your life, or if you want a free information packet for your school, please write me at:

Bill Sanders Speeches
P.O. Box 711
Portage, MI 49081